AIDS LAW

Third Edition

by
Margaret C. Jasper

Oceana's Legal Almanac Series:
Law for the Layperson

Oceana®
NEW YORK

OXFORD

UNIVERSITY PRESS

Oxford University Press, Inc., publishes works that further Oxford University's objective of excellence in research, scholarship, and education.

Copyright © 2008 by Oxford University Press, Inc.
Published by Oxford University Press, Inc.
198 Madison Avenue, New York, New York 10016

Oxford is a registered trademark of Oxford University Press
Oceana is a registered trademark of Oxford University Press, Inc.

Library of Congress Cataloging-in-Publication Data

Jasper, Margaret C.
    AIDS law / by Margaret C. Jasper. -- 3rd ed.
    p. cm. -- (Oceana's legal almanac series: law for the layperson)
    Includes bibliographical references.
    ISBN 978-0-19-537617-3 (alk. paper)   1. AIDS (Disease)--Law and legislation--United States--Popular works.   I. Title.
    KF3803.A54J37 2008
    344.73'04369792--dc22   2008010854

Note to Readers:

This publication is designed to provide accurate and authoritative information in regard to the subject matter covered. It is based upon sources believed to be accurate and reliable and is intended to be current as of the time it was written. It is sold with the understanding that the publisher is not engaged in rendering legal, accounting, or other professional services. If legal advice or other expert assistance is required, the services of a competent professional person should be sought. Also, to confirm that the information has not been affected or changed by recent developments, traditional legal research techniques should be used, including checking primary sources where appropriate.

(Based on the Declaration of Principles jointly adopted by a Committee of the American Bar Association and a Committee of Publishers and Associations.)

You may order this or any other Oxford University Press publication by visiting the Oxford University Press website at www.oup.com

To My Husband Chris

Your love and support

are my motivation and inspiration

To My Sons, Michael, Nick and Chris

-and-

In memory of my son, Jimmy

Table of Contents

ABOUT THE AUTHOR

MARGARET C. JASPER is an attorney engaged in the general practice of law in South Salem, New York, concentrating in the areas of personal injury and entertainment law. Ms. Jasper holds a Juris Doctor degree from Pace University School of Law, White Plains, New York, is a member of the New York and Connecticut bars, and is certified to practice before the United States District Courts for the Southern and Eastern Districts of New York, the United States Court of Appeals for the Second Circuit, and the United States Supreme Court.

Ms. Jasper has been appointed to the law guardian panel for the Family Court of the State of New York, is a member of a number of professional organizations and associations, and is a New York State licensed real estate broker operating as Jasper Real Estate, in South Salem, New York.

Margaret Jasper maintains a website at http://www.JasperLawOffice.com.

In 2004, Ms. Jasper successfully argued a case before the New York Court of Appeals, which gives mothers of babies who are stillborn due to medical negligence the right to bring a legal action and recover emotional distress damages. This successful appeal overturned a 26-year old New York case precedent, which previously prevented mothers of stillborn babies from suing their negligent medical providers.

Ms. Jasper is the author and general editor of the following legal Almanacs:

AIDS Law

The Americans with Disabilities Act

Animal Rights Law

Auto Leasing

Bankruptcy Law for the Individual Debtor

Banks and their Customers

Becoming a Citizen

Buying and Selling Your Home

Commercial Law

Consumer Rights and the Law

Co-ops and Condominiums: Your Rights and Obligations As Owner

Copyright Law

Credit Cards and the Law

Custodial Rights

Dealing with Debt

Dictionary of Selected Legal Terms

Drunk Driving Law

DWI, DUI and the Law

Education Law

Elder Law

Employee Rights in the Workplace

Employment Discrimination Under Title VII

Environmental Law

Estate Planning

Everyday Legal Forms

Executors and Personal Representatives: Rights and Responsibilities

Guardianship and the Law

Harassment in the Workplace

Health Care and Your Rights

Health Care Directives

Hiring Household Help and Contractors: Your Rights and Obligations
Under the Law

Home Mortgage Law Primer

Hospital Liability Law

How To Change Your Name

How To Form an LLC

How To Protect Your Challenged Child

How To Start Your Own Business

Identity Theft and How To Protect Yourself

Individual Bankruptcy and Restructuring

Injured on the Job: Employee Rights, Worker's Compensation and Disability Insurance Law

International Adoption

Juvenile Justice and Children's Law

Labor Law

Landlord-Tenant Law

Law for the Small Business Owner

The Law of Adoption

The Law of Attachment and Garnishment

The Law of Buying and Selling

The Law of Capital Punishment

The Law of Child Custody

The Law of Contracts

The Law of Debt Collection

The Law of Dispute Resolution

The Law of Immigration

The Law of Libel and Slander

The Law of Medical Malpractice

The Law of No-Fault Insurance

The Law of Obscenity and Pornography

The Law of Personal Injury

The Law of Premises Liability

The Law of Product Liability

The Law of Speech and the First Amendment

Lemon Laws

Living Together: Practical Legal Issues

Marriage and Divorce

Missing and Exploited Children: How to Protect Your Child

Motor Vehicle Law

Nursing Home Negligence

Patent Law

Pet Law

Planes, Trains and Buses: Your Rights as a Passenger

Prescription Drugs

Privacy and the Internet: Your Rights and Expectations Under the Law

Probate Law

Protecting Your Business: Disaster Preparation and the Law

Real Estate Law for the Homeowner and Broker

Religion and the Law

Retirement Planning

The Right to Die

Rights of Single Parents

Small Claims Court

Social Security Law

Special Education Law

Teenagers and Substance Abuse

Trademark Law

Trouble Next Door: What to do With Your Neighbor

Veterans Rights and Benefits

Victim's Rights Law

Violence Against Women

Welfare: Your Rights and the Law

What if It Happened to You: Violent Crimes and Victims' Rights

What if the Product Doesn't Work: Warranties & Guarantees

Workers' Compensation Law

Your Child's Legal Rights: An Overview

Your Rights in a Class Action Suit

Your Rights as a Tenant

Your Rights Under the Family and Medical Leave Act

You've Been Fired: Your Rights and Remedies

INTRODUCTION

This legal Almanac explores the area of law concerning Acquired Immune Deficiency Syndrome, a disease commonly known as AIDS, and the underlying virus (HIV) that causes AIDS. Ever since the appearance of AIDS in the United States in the early 1980s, the medical and political communities have been trying to develop a public policy that will protect the spread of this disease, while at the same time safeguard the afflicted individual's rights and liberties. This has been a difficult task, particularly given the devastating nature of the disease, and the rampant fear that has seized this nation.

This Almanac discusses the background and history of the disease, and current statistical information. Although the Almanac is not designed to be a medical treatise on the subject, it gives an overview of the medical aspects of HIV/AIDS, HIV testing options, and some of the common treatments being utilized to treat the disease. Controversial issues such as mandatory testing, name reporting and partnership notification are explored, as well as the criminal aspect of HIV transmission.

AIDS sufferers became the newest group to face all types of discrimination involving such important areas as employment, health care, education and housing. Advocates have been able to get critical legislation passed to combat this widespread intolerance, as more fully set forth in this Almanac. A discussion of the individual's legal rights in areas such as employment, education, health care, and insurance are also considered, as well as AIDS-related legislation.

Finally, the Almanac explores the rights of HIV/AIDS victims in the United States military and correctional settings.

The Appendix provides directories of organizations concerned with the rights of AIDS victims, applicable statutes, and other pertinent information and data. The Glossary contains definitions of many of the terms used throughout the Almanac.

CHAPTER 1:
HISTORICAL PERSPECTIVE

EARLY HISTORY—THE 1970s

AIDS is believed to have first surfaced in the mid-1970s in Central Africa. One of its earliest known victims was Dr. Grethe Rask, a surgeon who had worked in Zaire hospitals. Dr. Rask died in her native Denmark in 1977 from what doctors were calling a "mystery disease" that appeared to attack the immune system and cause a reduction in the number of disease fighting "T Cells" in the blood.

Dr. Rask's symptoms included weight loss, severe diarrhea, swollen lymph glands, fatigue, oral yeast infections, and breathing difficulties. She ultimately died of a rare form of pneumonia, known as *pneumocystis carinii,* which her immune system was unable to combat.

EMERGENCE OF AIDS IN THE UNITED STATES—THE 1980s

In 1980, similar symptoms began appearing in New York's homosexual community. Another seemingly related affliction, Kaposi's Sarcoma, was also noted to occur. Kaposi's Sarcoma is a rare form of skin cancer characterized by blue-violet to brownish lesions on various parts of the body.

The New York victims also suffered from a tremendous drop in their T-Cell count, which made them unable to fight off infections. These first known victims all died by the end of 1980, several of whom succumbed to *pneumocystis carinii* as did Dr. Rask.

In the following years, new cases of this "mystery disease" appeared in areas of the country with notably large homosexual communities. For this reason, it was mainly viewed as a "gay disease" until the symptoms began appearing in other groups, such as intravenous drug users and their children, Haitian immigrants and hemophiliacs.

Although the condition was not confined to the homosexual community, it was initially named Gay-Related Immune Deficiency (GRID). However, an outcry from gay organizations over the name given this immune system disease finally led to its redesignation as Acquired Immune Deficiency Syndrome (AIDS).

The Centers for Disease Control (CDC), based in Atlanta, struggled to come up with a cause for this unusual disease. Particularly due to its appearance in heterosexual hemophiliacs, the scientists feared that an unknown deadly virus was being transmitted through blood products.

A number of studies were undertaken to determine how the virus was transmitted. Progress was hampered due to limited funding. Because the victims were primarily homosexuals and drug addicts, public sympathy was lacking.

In 1981, a French Canadian flight attendant, Gaetan Dugas, was treated at the New York University Medical Center for Kaposi's Sarcoma. During his interview, he stated that he had numerous sexual encounters in both the United States and Canada. In 1982, researchers in California were able to determine that eight Los Angeles patients suffering from AIDS had either a sexual relationship with Mr. Dugas, or with one of his sexual partners. From this information, they were able to surmise that the virus could be transmitted through sexual relations. By tracking the data, the researchers also noted that the disease had a relatively long incubation period.

By this time, the CDC was receiving so many reported cases of AIDS, that they were treating it as an epidemic, and recommending that guidelines for blood donations be implemented. They were met with strong opposition from the blood suppliers, who felt that the evidence concerning transmission through blood transfusions was not sufficient to place such a costly burden on the system.

The CDC's suspicion that AIDS could be transmitted through blood transfusions was subsequently confirmed when a newborn who had received a number of blood transfusions following birth came down with symptoms of AIDS. It was discovered that one of the infant's blood donors had himself died of AIDS. Nevertheless, the blood suppliers were still opposed to the implementation of guidelines until stronger evidence was produced.

Once the media broadcast the story, the public became alarmed and questions concerning possible modes of transmission were raised. The CDC attempted to address these concerns by stating that the only known way AIDS could be transmitted was through blood and bodily fluids, e.g., semen. As the media coverage of AIDS increased, and celebrities and other notable figures publicly announced their affliction with the disease, funds for additional research were approved by Congress, and numerous fundraisers were held.

Researching and Tracking the Virus

Intensive research was undertaken, spearheaded in the United States by Dr. Robert Gallo, a leading scientist in the field of viral diseases, and in France by several prominent French scientists. In 1984, through their joint efforts, the deadly virus which causes AIDS was found, and was labeled HTLV-III—now commonly referred to as Human Immunodeficiency Virus (HIV).

The next step the scientists pursued was to trace the path of the deadly virus. Because there was such a large concentration of victims in Central Africa, the consensus among researchers was that the virus somehow originated in this area. Because AIDS is similar to a virus found in African monkeys, a theory developed that tribal hunters contracted the disease after being exposed to the blood of infected monkeys. The path of the virus is thought to have spread to Europe and Haiti by humans who had been in Central Africa, such as Dr. Rask.

PRESENT DAY

During the 1990s, the AIDS epidemic shifted steadily toward a growing proportion of cases in blacks and Hispanics and in women, and a decrease in the proportion of homosexual men, although according to the CDC, this group remains the largest single exposure group. In absolute numbers, blacks have outnumbered whites in new AIDS diagnoses and deaths since 1996, and in the number of persons living with AIDS since 1998. The proportion of women with AIDS has also increased steadily, reaching 23% in 1999. The proportion of individuals infected heterosexually has also increased and, in 1994, surpassed the proportion of individuals infected through injection drug use.

In the mid-1990s, due to the development and availability of more effective therapies, the number of AIDS deaths started to decrease. However, according to the CDC, as deaths caused by AIDS has decreased, the prevalence of AIDS has steadily increased year to year. The CDC expects that this trend will continue as long as the number of persons with a new AIDS diagnoses exceeds the number of persons dying each year.

AIDS ORGANIZATIONS AND RESOURCES

A number of organizations have emerged which were started by individuals who were concerned over the AIDS crisis. Such organizations offer various services to victims of the disease, including legal services, counseling, housing, and medical care.

A number of these organizations provide valuable information on the Internet, and also provide links to other websites that contain an enormous amount of information and resources on the disease.

An HIV/AIDS resource directory is set forth in Appendix 1 and a directory of government agencies concerned with HIV/AIDS issues is set forth in Appendix 2.

THE NATIONAL ASSOCIATION OF PEOPLE WITH AIDS (NAPWA)

Founded in 1983, the National Association of People With AIDS (NAPWA) is the oldest coalition of people living with HIV/AIDS in the world and the oldest national AIDS organization. NAPWA advocates on behalf of all people living with HIV and AIDS in order to end the pandemic and human suffering caused by HIV/AIDS. HIV-positive people have a unique role to play in HIV prevention and promotion of voluntary HIV counseling and testing.

National HIV Testing Day

NAPWA sponsors the National HIV Testing Day (NHTD), an annual campaign to encourage at-risk individuals to receive voluntary HIV counseling and testing. Across the country, thousands of HIV counseling and testing sites, state and local health departments, and community-based HIV/AIDS service providers participate in NHTD events, by holding health fairs, providing community and media outreach, hosting special testing-related events or operating extended hours. Support of some NHTD activities is provided by federal and corporate sponsors.

NHTD organizers reach out to communities at increased risk of HIV infection, including African American and Latino populations, both of which are disproportionately affected with HIV when compared to other demographic groups in the United States.

Information regarding National HIV Testing Day may be obtained by contacting NAPWA:

> Telephone: 240-247-0880
>
> E-mail: NHTD@NAPWA.org
>
> Website: www.napwa.org

AIDS HOTLINES

The Centers for Disease Control and Prevention (CDC) operates a toll-free National AIDS Hotline that is open 24 hours a day, 7 days a week.

The Hotline was established in February 1983 as one of the first government services established to respond to the public's questions about the AIDS epidemic. The Hotline is presently the world's largest health information service, receiving an average of about 3,000 calls each day. To date, over 13 million calls have been handled by the Hotline.

The Hotline offers anonymous, confidential HIV/AIDS information to the American public. Trained information specialists answer questions about HIV infection and AIDS in English (1-800-342-AIDS) and Spanish (1-800-344-7432), and provide TTY service for the deaf (1-800-243- 7889).

The Hotline also provide referrals to appropriate services, including clinics, hospitals, local hotlines, counseling and testing sites, legal services, health departments, support groups, educational organizations, and service agencies throughout the United States. Callers can also order various publications, posters, and other informational materials from the CDC National Prevention Information Network through the Hotline.

In addition to the National AIDS Hotline, every state has its own AIDS hotline which provides information and referrals.

A Directory of State AIDS Hotlines is set forth in Appendix 3.

THE NAMES PROJECT FOUNDATION

The NAMES Project Foundation was started in 1987 by a small group of individuals, many of whom had suffered loss of friends and loved ones to AIDS. They were intent on making sure that those who died from this devastating disease would not easily be forgotten. Their message is expressed in the AIDS Memorial Quilt.

The idea of making a patchwork quilt memorial to AIDS victims was initially conceived by Cleve Jones, a San Francisco gay rights activist. Mr. Jones was largely responsible for organizing an annual candlelight march in San Francisco. The march was dedicated to the memory of two gay men: Mayor George Moscone and Supervisor Harvey Milk, both of whom had been assassinated in 1978.

In preparation for the 1985 march, Mr. Jones noted that over one thousand San Francisco citizens had lost their lives to AIDS. Thus, he thought it appropriate to have each of the marchers write the names of friends and loved ones who had died of the disease on placards. Following the march, the placards were taped to the wall of the San Francisco Federal Building. The placards on the wall looked very much like a patchwork quilt to Mr. Jones, thus, The Aids Memorial Quilt was born.

Mr. Jones was responsible for creating the first panel for the AIDS Memorial Quilt in 1986, in memory of a close friend. He and other members of his group formed the NAMES Project Foundation in 1987 to continue the effort. They received a lot of support from the public, both in materials and volunteer work. The Foundation started receiving hundreds of panels from friends and loved ones of AIDS victims throughout the world.

The AIDS Memorial Quilt was first publicly displayed on October 11, 1987 on the National Mall in Washington, D.C. The unveiling took place during the National March on Washington for Lesbian and Gay Rights. The dimensions of the quilt were quite impressive by that time. It was larger than a football field and encompassed 1,920 panels, each measuring 3 feet by 6 feet.

The AIDS Memorial Quilt was subsequently taken on its first national tour in 1988, in an effort to raise funding for AIDS organizations. By the end of the four-month tour, the quilt had grown to over 6,000 panels. Since that time, the quilt has been displayed a number of times, each time increasing in size and raising additional funds for AIDS-related services and research. A tradition began which includes a reading of the panel names each time the quilt is displayed. In 1989, the AIDS Memorial Quilt was nominated for a Nobel Peace Prize, and was the subject of an Academy Award winning feature length documentary film entitled "Common Threads: Stories From The Quilt."

By 1992, the AIDS Memorial Quilt included panels from every state and 28 countries. In January 1993, the NAMES Project was invited to march in President Clinton's inaugural parade. The last display of the entire AIDS Memorial Quilt was in October of 1996 when the quilt covered the entire National Mall in Washington, D.C.

As more lives succumb to the deadly disease, the quilt continues to grow, and has become the largest ongoing community arts project in the world. Panels have been contributed by over 35 countries, all 50 states, Washington D.C., Guam, and Puerto Rico.

At last count, the AIDS Memorial Quilt included more than 46,000 panels, 91,000 names, spanned 1,293,300 square feet, and weighed more than 54 tons. The quilt would measure 52.5 miles long if all of the 3' by 6' panels were laid end to end. There are over 91,000 names included on the quilt, which represents approximately 17.5% of all AIDS deaths in the United States.

Due to its massive size, the quilt can no longer be displayed in its entirety, but portions of the quilt continue to tour the world. Since 1987, over 15,200,000 people have visited the quilt at thousands of displays worldwide and over $4 million dollars have been raised by the NAMES Project Foundation designated for direct services for people with AIDS.

In support of the effort to continue this remarkable visual memorial to those who have lost their lives to AIDS, and to raise money for AIDS research and treatment, there are approximately 18 NAMES Project chapters in the United States and 43 international affiliates.

Contributing a Panel for the AIDS Quilt

In order to add a name to the Aids Quilt, you must make a panel. The Names Project Foundation website (http://aidsquilt.org/) provides details on how to create your own panel. Basically, you must include the name of the person you want to remember, and any additional information about the person, such as their date of birth and death, etc. The material you choose should be durable because the quilt is often folded and unfolded when it is on display. The finished, hemmed panel must be exactly 3 feet by 6 feet.

When you submit your panel, you should include a letter about the person you want remembered, and include a photograph for the NAMES Project Foundation archives. Although there is no cost for adding a panel to the quilt, a donation in any amount is appreciated, if possible, to help pay for the cost of adding the panel. In addition, you must fill out the panel maker information form and send it along with the panel.

A sample AIDS Quilt Panel Maker Information Form is set forth at Appendix 4.

Once completed, there are several ways to submit the panel and supporting documents to the NAMES Project Foundation:

1. Send the panel by Registered Mail or Carrier that can track the package (Federal Express, UPS, etc.) to:

The NAMES Project Foundation

637 Hoke Street NW

Atlanta, GA 30318-4315

Attn: New Panels

2. Bring the panel to a Quilt Display.

3. Bring the panel to one of the NAMES Project Foundation Chapter offices.

The entire process, from receipt of the panel to inclusion in the AIDS Quilt, typically takes between 90 days and six months.

Readers can obtain additional information about the NAMES Project Foundation and the AIDS Memorial Quilt, and view quilt panels on-line at their website (http://aidsquilt.org).

Directories of the NAMES Project Foundation Chapters and NAMES Project International Affiliates are set forth at Appendices 5 and 6, respectively.

THE RYAN WHITE CARE ACT

In 1990, in an effort to ease the increased demand on the already over-burdened public health infrastructure due to the HIV/AIDS epidemic, the Legislature enacted the Ryan White Comprehensive AIDS Resources Emergency (CARE) Act. The Ryan White CARE Act represents the Federal Government's largest financial allocation specifically for HIV-related health and support services.

The CARE Act was passed in memory of Ryan White, a teenager who contracted AIDS through a tainted hemophilia treatment in 1984. Ryan was expelled from school after contracting the disease. Thereafter, he became an advocate for AIDS research and awareness until his death in 1990.

The CARE Act provides funding to states and other public or private non-profit organizations to develop, organize, coordinate and operate more effective and cost-efficient systems for the delivery of essential health care and support services to medically underserved individuals and families affected by AIDS/HIV. A significant portion of funding from the act is emergency relief for eligible metropolitan areas.

CARE Act funds are used to provide primary medical care, AIDS drugs, viral load testing, treatment information, support, case management, and other essential support services for tens of thousands of individuals living with HIV/AIDS. The CARE Act has dramatically improved the quality of life for people living with HIV/AIDS and their families; reduced the use of costly inpatient care; and increased access to care for under-served populations, including minority groups. The CARE Act has also reduced the need for expensive hospitalization or skilled nursing home care for people with AIDS.

The CARE Act was reauthorized in 2006 for three years, until September 2009, with a funding level of $2.1 billion dollars. Prior to reauthorization, the Act allocated money based on the proportion of patients with full-blown AIDS in each region. The reauthorized Act changed this provision and includes the number of people with HIV infection in the allocation of funds. In addition, the reauthorized Act redefined the eligible metropolitan areas as cities with a population greater than 50,000 instead of 500,000, as per the previous version of the Act.

CHAPTER 2:
HIV/AIDS STATISTICS

HIV/AIDS SURVEILLANCE REPORTS

The HIV/AIDS epidemic was first recognized in the United States in 1981. Since that time, all 50 states and the 5 U.S. dependent areas (American Samoa, Guam, the Northern Mariana Islands, Puerto Rico, and the U.S. Virgin Islands) have conducted AIDS surveillance using a standardized, confidential, name-based reporting system. Each year, the Centers for Disease Control and Prevention (CDC) publishes an HIV/AIDS Surveillance Report. The report contains data reported to the CDC for cases of HIV infection and AIDS diagnoses.

The 50 states also publish individual surveillance reports concerning the incidence of HIV infection and AIDS diagnoses reported within their jurisdiction.

A table setting forth the web addresses for the state HIV/AIDS surveillance reports is set forth in Appendix 7.

REPORTING AREAS

The data gathered by the CDC is based on statistics collected from 37 reporting areas that have conducted confidential name-based HIV infection information long enough (since at least 2001) to be able to adequately monitor trends. These 37 areas include 33 states and 4 U.S. dependent areas.

The 33 reporting states include Alabama, Alaska, Arizona, Arkansas, Colorado, Florida, Idaho, Indiana, Iowa, Kansas, Louisiana, Michigan, Minnesota, Mississippi, Missouri, Nebraska, Nevada, New Jersey, New Mexico, New York, North Carolina, North Dakota, Ohio, Oklahoma, South Carolina, South Dakota, Tennessee, Texas, Utah, Virginia, West Virginia, Wisconsin, and Wyoming. These 33 states represent approximately 63% of the epidemic in the United States.

The 4 reporting U.S. dependent areas include American Samoa, Guam, the Northern Mariana Islands, and the U.S. Virgin Islands.

As set forth below, the 2005 HIV/AIDS Surveillance Report, the most recently published report, contains the following data:

1. Cases of HIV/AIDS. This refers to cases of HIV infection, regardless of whether they have progressed to AIDS;

2. AIDS deaths;

3. Persons living with HIV/AIDS, AIDS, or HIV infection (not AIDS);

4. Survival rates after diagnosis; and

5. Reports of cases of HIV/AIDS, AIDS, and HIV infections (not AIDS).

HIV/AIDS CASES AND AIDS CASES

According to Section 1 of the 2005 HIV/AIDS Surveillance Report, the following statistics reflect: (1) the number of cases of HIV/AIDS, regardless of whether the cases have progressed to AIDS; and (2) the number of AIDS cases, by selected characteristics and year of diagnosis.

HIV/AIDS Cases

From 2001 through 2004, the total number of new cases of HIV/AIDS in the 33 reporting states decreased slightly, and then increased in 2005. HIV/AIDS prevalence—i.e., the number of persons living with HIV/AIDS—increased during this time.

At the end of 2005, an estimated 475,220 persons in the 33 reporting states had been given a diagnosis and were living with HIV/AIDS. The estimated rate of HIV/AIDS cases in the 33 reporting states was 19.8 per 100,000 persons.

Of all the HIV infections diagnosed in 2004 in the 33 reporting states, 39% were diagnosed with AIDS less than 12 months after HIV infection was diagnosed. AIDS was diagnosed less than 12 months after the diagnosis of HIV infection for larger proportions of persons aged 35 years and older, and for injection drug users (IDUs).

Age Groups

From 2001 through 2005, the estimated number of HIV/AIDS cases decreased among children less than 13 years of age, as well as persons in the following age groups: (1) 13–14; (2) 30–34; (3) 35–39; (4) 40–44; and (5) 45–49.

The estimated number of HIV/AIDS cases remained stable among persons 65 years and older, and increased among persons in the following age groups: (1) 15–19; (2) 20–24; (3) 25–29; (4) 50–54; and (5) 55–59.

The largest number of HIV/AIDS cases occurred among persons aged 35–39, and accounted for 16% of all HIV/AIDS cases diagnosed in 2005.

Race/Ethnicity

From 2001 through 2005, the estimated number of HIV/AIDS cases increased among whites, Asian/Pacific Islanders, and American Indians/ Alaska Natives, and decreased among blacks and Hispanics. Blacks accounted for 49% of all HIV/AIDS cases diagnosed in 2005.

In 2005, rates of HIV/AIDS cases were 71.3 per 100,000 in the Black population; 27.8 per 100,000 in the Hispanic population; 10.4 per 100,000 in the American Indian/Alaska Native population; 8.8 per 100,000 in the White population, and 7.4 per 100,000 in the Asian/ Pacific Islander population.

Sex

From 2001 through 2005, the estimated number of HIV/AIDS cases decreased approximately 1% among males and 19% among females. In 2005, males accounted for 73% of all HIV/AIDS cases among adults and adolescents.

Transmission Category

From 2001 through 2005, the estimated number of HIV/AIDS cases increased among men who have sex with men (MSM). The estimated number of HIV/AIDS cases decreased among injection drug users (IDUs), MSM who were also IDUs, adults and adolescents who have high-risk heterosexual contact, and among children. MSM (49%) and persons exposed through high-risk heterosexual contact (32%) accounted for 81% of all HIV/AIDS cases diagnosed in 2005.

AIDS Cases

From 2001 through 2005, the estimated number of AIDS cases increased approximately 7%. In 2005, the estimated rate of AIDS cases in the 50 states and the District of Columbia was 13.7 per 100,000.

Age Groups

From 2001 through 2005, the estimated number of AIDS cases decreased 44% among children less than 13 years of age. The estimated number of AIDS cases also decreased among persons in the following age groups: (1) 30–34 and (2) 35–39.

The estimated number of AIDS cases increased among persons in the following age groups: (1) 15–19; (2) 20–24; (3) 25–29; (4) 40–44; (5) 45–49; (6) 50–54; (7) 55–59; (8) 60–65; and (9) 65 years and older. The largest number of AIDS cases occurred among persons aged 40–44 and accounted for 20% of all AIDS cases diagnosed in 2005 in the 50 states and the District of Columbia.

A table setting forth the estimated number of AIDS cases, by age at diagnosis and year of diagnosis, in the 50 states and the District of Columbia (2001–2005), is set forth in Appendix 8.

Race/Ethnicity

From 2001 through 2005, the estimated number of AIDS cases increased among all racial and ethnic groups. In 2005, rates of AIDS cases were 54.1 per 100,000 in the Black population; 18.0 per 100,000 in the Hispanic population; 7.4 per 100,000 in the American Indian/Alaska Native population; 5.9 per 100,000 in the White population, and 3.6 per 100,000 in the Asian/Pacific Islander population.

A table setting forth the estimated number of AIDS cases, by race/ethnicity and year of diagnosis, in the 50 states and the District of Columbia (2001–2005), is set forth in Appendix 9.

Sex

From 2001 through 2005, the estimated number of AIDS cases increased 7% among females and 7% among males. Males accounted for 73% of all AIDS cases diagnosed in 2005 among adults and adolescents in the 50 states and the District of Columbia. Rates of AIDS cases in 2005 were 24.9 per 100,000 among males and 8.6 per 100,000 among females.

Transmission Category

From 2001 through 2005, among male adults and adolescents, the estimated number of AIDS cases decreased among IDUs and MSM who were also IDUs, and increased among MSM and males exposed through high-risk heterosexual contact.

Among female adults and adolescents, from 2001 through 2005, the estimated number of AIDS cases decreased among IDUs and increased among females exposed through high-risk heterosexual contact.

A table setting forth the estimated number of AIDS cases, by transmission category (male) and transmission category (female) and year of diagnosis, in the 50 states and the District of Columbia (2001–2005), is set forth in Appendices 10 and 11, respectively.

Region

From 2001 through 2005, the estimated number of AIDS cases increased 24% in the Midwest, 9% in the South, and 2% in the Northeast. The number of cases decreased 3% in the West.

A table setting forth the estimated number of AIDS deaths, by region of residence and year of diagnosis, in the 50 states and the District of Columbia (2001–2005), is set forth in Appendix 12.

A table setting forth the top 10 states/dependent areas with the highest number of AIDS cases (2005) is set forth in Appendix 13.

A table setting forth the top 10 states/dependent areas with the highest cumulative number of AIDS cases (through 2005) is set forth in Appendix 14.

AIDS DEATHS

According to Section 2 of the 2005 HIV/AIDS Surveillance Report, the following statistics reflect the number of deaths attributed to AIDS, by selected characteristics and year of diagnosis. The estimated number of deaths of persons from AIDS who resided in the 50 states and the District of Columbia decreased 4% from 2001 through 2005.

Age Groups

From 2001 through 2005, the estimated number of AIDS deaths decreased among children less than 13 years of age, and in the following age groups: (1) 20–24; (2) 25–29; (3) 30–34; (4) 35–39; and (5) 40–44.

The estimated number of AIDS deaths remained stable among persons aged 15–19 years, and increased in the following age groups: (1) 13–14; (2) 45–49; (3) 50–54; (4) 55–59; (5) 60–64; and (6) 65 years and older.

A table setting forth the estimated number of AIDS cases, by age at death and year of death, in the 50 states and the District of Columbia (2001–2005), is set forth in Appendix 15.

Race/Ethnicity

From 2001 through 2005, the estimated number of AIDS deaths decreased among Whites and Blacks. The estimated number of AIDS deaths remained stable among Hispanics, Asians/Pacific Islanders, and American Indians/Alaska Natives.

A table setting forth the estimated number of AIDS deaths, by race/ethnicity and year of death, in the 50 states and the District of Columbia (2001–2005), is set forth in Appendix 16.

Sex/Transmission Category

From 2001 through 2005, both among males and females, the estimated number of AIDS deaths of IDUs decreased, but the number of AIDS deaths of persons exposed through high-risk heterosexual contact increased.

A table setting forth the estimated number of AIDS deaths, by transmission category (male) and transmission category (female) and year of death, in the 50 states and the District of Columbia (2001–2005), is set forth in Appendices 17 and 18, respectively.

Region

From 2001 through 2005, the estimated number of AIDS deaths decreased in the Northeast, Midwest, and West, and increased in the South.

A table setting forth the estimated number of AIDS deaths, by region of residence and year of death, in the 50 states and the District of Columbia (2001–2005), is set forth in Appendix 19.

PERSONS LIVING WITH HIV/AIDS, HIV INFECTION (NOT AIDS) OR AIDS

According to Section 3 of the 2005 HIV/AIDS Surveillance Report, the following statistics reflect the number of persons living with HIV/AIDS, HIV Infection (Not AIDS) or AIDS, by selected characteristics and year of diagnosis.

Persons Living With HIV/AIDS

From 2001 through 2005, the estimated number of persons living with HIV/AIDS increased steadily in the 33 reporting states. At the end of 2005, an estimated 475,220 persons were living with HIV/AIDS in the 33 reporting states since 2001.

Age Groups

From 2001 through 2005, the largest estimated number of persons living with HIV/AIDS (21%) was among persons aged 40–44.

Race/Ethnicity

From 2001 through 2005, among the estimated number of persons living with HIV/AIDS, 47% were Black; 34% were White; 17% were Hispanic; and less than 1% each were American Indian/Alaska Native or Asian/Pacific Islander.

Sex

From 2001 through 2005, 73% of adults and adolescents living with HIV/AIDS were male.

Transmission Category

From 2001 through 2005, of the estimated 341,524 male adults and adolescents living with HIV/AIDS, 61% had been exposed through male-to-male sexual contact; 18% had been exposed through injection drug use; and 13% had been exposed through both male-to-male sexual contact and injection drug use.

Of the estimated 126,964 female adults and adolescents living with HIV/AIDS, 72% had been exposed through high-risk heterosexual contact, and 26% had been exposed through injection drug use.

Of the estimated 6,726 children living with HIV/AIDS, 90% had been exposed perinatally.

Persons Living With HIV Infection (Not AIDS)

Since 2001, the prevalence rate of HIV infection (not AIDS) in the 33 reporting states and 4 reporting U.S. dependent areas among adults and adolescents was estimated at 137 per 100,000 at the end of 2005. The prevalence rate of HIV infection (not AIDS) among children residing in the same 37 reporting areas was estimated at 7.4 per 100,000 at the end of 2005.

Persons Living With AIDS

Since 2001, the prevalence of AIDS has also increased steadily. At the end of 2005, an estimated 421,873 persons in the 50 states and the District of Columbia were living with AIDS.

Age Groups

By the end of 2005, the largest estimated number of persons living with AIDS (23%) was among persons aged 40–44.

A table setting forth the estimated number of persons living with AIDS, by age and year, in the 50 states and the District of Columbia (2001–2005), is set forth in Appendix 20.

Race/Ethnicity

By the end of 2005, among the estimated number of persons living with AIDS, 44% were Black; 35% were White; 19% were Hispanic; 1% were Asian/Pacific Islander; and less than 1% each were American Indian/Alaska Native.

A table setting forth the estimated number of persons living with AIDS, by race/ethnicity and year, in the 50 states and the District of Columbia (2001–2005), is set forth in Appendix 21.

Sex

By the end of 2005, 77% of adults and adolescents living with AIDS were male.

Transmission Category

By the end of 2005, of the estimated 322,125 male adults and adolescents living with AIDS, 59% had been exposed through male-to-male sexual contact; 20% had been exposed through injection drug use; 11% had been exposed through high-risk heterosexual contact; and 8% had been exposed through both male-to-male sexual contact and injection drug use.

Of the estimated 95,959 female adults and adolescents living with HIV/ AIDS, 65% had been exposed through high-risk heterosexual contact; and 33% had been exposed through injection drug use.

A table setting forth the estimated number of persons living with AIDS, by transmission category (male), transmission category (female), transmission category (child under 13) and year, in the 50 states and the District of Columbia (2001–2005), is set forth in Appendix 22, 23 and 24, respectively.

Region

By the end of 2005, 40% of persons living with AIDS resided in the South; 30% in the Northeast; 20% in the West; and 11% in the Midwest.

A table setting forth the estimated number of persons living with AIDS, by region of residence and year, in the 50 states and the District of Columbia (2001–2005), is set forth in Appendix 25.

SURVIVAL RATES AFTER AIDS DIAGNOSIS

According to Section 4 of the 2005 HIV/AIDS Surveillance Report, the following statistics reflect the survival rates of persons surviving a given length of time after being diagnosed with AIDS, by selected characteristics and year of diagnosis.

Survival increased with the year of diagnosis for diagnoses made during 1997–1999. Year-to-year differences were small during 2000–2004.

Age Groups

Survival rates decreased as age at diagnosis increased among persons at least 35 years old at diagnosis and in comparison with persons younger than 35. Survival rates were similar for the age groups 13–24 and 25–34. Survival rates were greatest among children less than 13 years of age at diagnosis.

Race/Ethnicity

Survival rates, particularly at more than 48 months after diagnosis, were greater among Asians/Pacific Islanders, whites, and Hispanics, than among blacks. Results were unstable or inconsistent for American Indians/Alaska Natives because the numbers of persons in this racial/ ethnic category were small.

Transmission Category

Survival rates were greatest among MSM and among children with perinatally acquired HIV infection. Survival rates were intermediate among male and female adults and adolescents who had heterosexual contact with someone known to be HIV infected or at high risk for HIV infection, as well as among MSM who also were IDUs. Survival rates were lowest among male and female adults and adolescents who were IDUs.

REPORTS OF CASES OF HIV/AIDS, AIDS, AND HIV INFECTION (NOT AIDS)

According to Section 5 of the 2005 HIV/AIDS Surveillance Report, the following statistics reflect reports of cases of HIV/AIDS, AIDS, and HIV Infection (not AIDS).

Reports of AIDS Cases

Through 2005, a total of 956,019 persons in the United States had been reported as having AIDS. Three states (California, Florida, and New York) reported 43% of the cumulative AIDS cases, and 37% of AIDS cases reported to the Centers for Disease Control and Prevention (CDC) in 2005.

In the United States, the rate of reported AIDS cases in 2005 was 14.0 per 100,000 population. The rate of reported AIDS cases ranged from zero per 100,000 (American Samoa and the Commonwealth of Northern Mariana Islands) to 128.4 per 100,000 (District of Columbia).

By sex, in 2005, males accounted for 74% and females for 26% of 41,900 reported AIDS cases among adults and adolescents.

In 2005, 93 AIDS cases in children were reported.

Reports of Cases of HIV Infection (Not AIDS)

In 2005, 70% of the 35,107 reported cases of HIV infection (not AIDS) among adults and adolescents were in males, and 30% were in females.

In 2005, 430 cases of HIV infection (not AIDS) in children were reported.

INTERNATIONAL STATISTICS

According to estimates from the UNAIDS/WHO AIDS Epidemic Update issued in November 2007, approximately 30.8 million adults and 2.5 million children were living with HIV at the end of 2007. During 2007, approximately 2.5 million people became infected with HIV.

In addition, during this same time period, 2.1 million people died from AIDS. According to the statistics, the number of global deaths caused by AIDS peaked around 2005, but has since declined only slightly, despite the availability of antiretroviral (ARV) therapy.

A table setting forth the estimated number of global HIV/AIDS diagnoses and AIDS deaths (2007) is set forth in Appendix 26.

Age Groups

Approximately half of those persons who acquire HIV become infected before they turn 25 and typically die of AIDS before their 35th birthday. By the end of 2005, the epidemic had left behind 15.2 million "AIDS orphans"—i.e., children under the age of 18 who have lost one or both parents to AIDS. In 2007, approximately 420,000 children aged 14 or younger became infected with HIV.

Transmission Category

Globally, approximately 11% of HIV infections are among babies who acquire the virus from their mothers. Over 90% of newly infected children are babies born to HIV-positive women, who acquire the virus during pregnancy, labor or delivery, or through their mother's breast milk. Almost 90% of such transmissions occur in sub-Saharan Africa.

Additionally, 10% of HIV infections result from injection drug use; 5–10% are due to men having sex with men; and 5–10% occur in healthcare settings. Heterosexual sex accounts for the remaining two–thirds of new infections.

Regional Statistics

Globally, approximately 95% of HIV-infected people live in the developing world, which may be attributed to the lack of resources for prevention and proper health care, and overwhelming poverty in these areas. The greatest number of people living with AIDS is in countries with the highest incomes. This is likely due to the availability of life-prolonging antiretroviral (ARV) therapy in these areas.

Asia

Approximately 4.8 million people in Asia are living with HIV/AIDS. In 2006, it was estimated that there were approximately 5.7 million HIV-infected people in India. However, in July 2007, due to better data reporting, this estimate was revised downward to between 2 and 3.1 million. Other countries with large populations of HIV-infected people include China (650,000); Thailand (580,000); and Myanmar (360,000).

Of the Asian total, approximately 4 million people in South and South-East Asia are living with HIV/AIDS. Approximately 340,000 people became infected with the virus in 2007. The number of deaths from AIDS was estimated to be around 270,000 in 2007.

Of the Asian total, approximately 800,000 people in East Asia are living with HIV/AIDS. Approximately 92,000 people became infected with the virus in 2007. The number of deaths from AIDS was estimated to be around 32,000 in 2007.

Eastern Europe and Central Asia

Approximately 1.6 million people in Eastern Europe and Asia are living with HIV/AIDS, where the epidemic is reportedly experiencing a rapid increase. Approximately 150,000 people became infected with the virus in 2007. The number of deaths from AIDS were estimated to be around 55,000 in 2007, in large part due to the lack of antiretroviral (ARV) therapy.

The country with the largest population of HIV-infected people is the Russian Federation, where approximately 940,000 people are living with the virus. Other areas with large HIV-infected populations include the Ukraine; the Baltic states of Estonia, Latvia, and Lithuania, with more recent epidemics affecting Kyrgyzstan and Uzbekistan.

Latin America and the Caribbean

Approximately 1.6 million people in Latin America are living with HIV/AIDS. Approximately 100,000 people became infected with the virus in 2007. The number of deaths from AIDS was estimated to be around 58,000 in 2007.

Approximately 230,000 people in the Caribbean are living with HIV/AIDS. Approximately 17,000 people became infected with the virus in 2007. The number of deaths from AIDS was estimated to be around 11,000 in 2007.

The country with the largest population of HIV-infected people is Brazil, where approximately 620,000 people are living with the virus, although the death rate has decreased due to access to treatment. In Haiti and the Bahamas, adult prevalence of HIV is more than 3%, which is the highest incidence rate outside of Sub-Saharan Africa.

North Africa and the Middle East

Approximately 380,000 people in North Africa and the Middle East are living with HIV/AIDS. Approximately 35,000 people became infected with the virus in 2007. The number of deaths from AIDS was estimated to be around 25,000 in 2007.

North America

Approximately 1.3 million people in North America are living with HIV/AIDS. Approximately 46,000 people became infected with the virus in 2007. The number of deaths from AIDS was estimated to be around 21,000 in 2007.

Oceania

Approximately 75,000 people in Oceania are living with HIV/AIDS. Approximately 14,000 people became infected with the virus in 2007. The number of deaths from AIDS was estimated to be around 1,200 in 2007.

Sub-Saharan Africa

The worst HIV/AIDS epidemic in the world exists in the area of Africa south of the Sahara desert known as Sub-Saharan Africa. Approximately 22.5 million people in this area are living with HIV/AIDS. Approximately 1.7 million adults and children became infected with the virus in 2007. The number of deaths from AIDS was estimated to be around 1.6 million in 2007, in large part due to the lack of antiretroviral (ARV) therapy.

Although this region has just over 10% of the world's population, 68% of all people living with HIV/AIDS are located there. Nevertheless, the prevalence of HIV varies considerably across the region, e.g., ranging from less than 1% in Madagascar to over 30% in Swaziland.

Although the proportion of people living with HIV/AIDS in this region has decreased in recent years, this is reportedly due to the fact that the number of deaths each year exceeds the number of new infections. Nevertheless, there is still an increase in the total number of people living with HIV/AIDS due to the overall population growth.

Western and Central Europe

Approximately 760,000 people are living with HIV/AIDS in Western and Central Europe. Approximately 31,000 people became infected with the virus in 2007. The number of deaths from AIDS was estimated to be around 12,000 in 2007.

CHAPTER 3:
THE MEDICAL ASPECTS OF HIV/AIDS

THE HUMAN IMMUNODEFICIENCY VIRUS (HIV)

HIV is the acronym for Human Immunodeficiency Virus, the virus that causes AIDS. The "H" for *human*, means that the virus infects human beings. The "I" for *immunodeficiency,* means that the virus attacks a person's immune system. The immune system is the body's defense against infections, such as bacteria and viruses. Once HIV attacks the immune system, it becomes deficient and doesn't work properly. The "V" for *virus* refers to a type of germ too small to be seen even with a microscope.

Although some viruses stay in the body for a short period of time, such as a cold or flu, HIV does not "go away." A person who is infected with HIV is said to be "HIV-positive" or "HIV-infected." Once a person is HIV-positive, he or she will always be HIV-positive, unless and until a cure is found.

Transmission of the HIV Virus

HIV is presently believed to enter the blood stream through direct exchange of blood or blood products, and semen and vaginal secretions during sexual contact. Sexual contact that can transmit HIV includes: (1) vaginal sex; (2) anal sex; and (3) oral sex. Thus, experts advise that sexually active persons practice safe sex at all times.

A blood-borne HIV infection can occur through: (1) sharing needles when injecting drugs; (2) tattoos or body piercings using unsterilized needles; (3) accidental needle sticks; (4) blood transfusions; and (5) splashing blood in one's eyes.

In addition, HIV-infected pregnant women can pass HIV to their babies during pregnancy or delivery, as well as through breast-feeding. Taking anti-HIV drugs during pregnancy and childbirth can help lower this risk. New mothers are also advised to bottle-feed their newborns.

The body fluids that have been proven to spread HIV include blood; semen; vaginal fluid; breast milk; and other bodily fluids containing blood. Additional body fluids that health care workers may come into contact with, and which may transmit the virus, include cerebrospinal fluid surrounding the brain and the spinal cord; synovial fluid surrounding bone joints; and amniotic fluid surrounding a fetus.

Known victims of the disease have included individuals who received tainted blood, such as hemophiliacs; health care workers who have come in contact with infected blood; intravenous drug users who have shared needles with infected persons; and persons who have engaged in certain unprotected sexual activities. Thus, this disease is not limited to homosexuals or drug addicts as once believed.

Although HIV has been detected in saliva, scientists claim that it cannot be transmitted in that manner—i.e., by kissing—unless infected blood is able to pass through a sore or cut in the uninfected partner's mouth. However, according to the CDC, prolonged open-mouth kissing could damage the mouth or lips and allow HIV to pass from an infected person to a partner and then enter the body through cuts or sores in the mouth. Because of this possible risk, the CDC recommends against open-mouth kissing with an infected partner. One case suggests that a woman became infected with HIV from her sex partner through exposure to contaminated blood during open-mouth kissing.

Researchers have also stated that the virus cannot be spread by insect bites, e.g. mosquitoes, tears, sweat, feces or urine. According to the CDC, there has been no evidence of HIV transmission through mosquitoes or any other insects—even in areas where there are many cases of AIDS and large populations of mosquitoes. Lack of such outbreaks, despite intense efforts to detect them, supports the conclusion that HIV is not transmitted by insects.

The results of experiments and observations of insect biting behavior indicate that when an insect bites a person, it does not inject its own or a previously bitten person's or animal's blood into the next person bitten. Rather, it injects saliva, which acts as a lubricant so the insect can feed efficiently. Diseases such as yellow fever and malaria are transmitted through the saliva of specific species of mosquitoes. However, HIV lives for only a short time inside an insect and, unlike organisms that are transmitted via insect bites, HIV does not reproduce in insects. Thus, even if the virus enters a mosquito or another insect, the insect does not become infected and cannot transmit HIV to the next human it bites.

All viruses, including HIV, must infect living cells to reproduce. HIV takes over certain immune system cells that are supposed to defend the body. These cells are called CD4 cells, or T cells. When HIV takes over a CD4 cell, the cell produces thousands of copies of the virus. These copies infect other CD4 cells. The infected cells do not work and die early. Over time, the loss of the CD4 cells weakens the immune system, making it harder for the body to remain healthy.

People with HIV have what is called HIV infection. Many of these people will develop AIDS as a result of their HIV infection. However, a positive HIV test result does not mean that a person has AIDS. A diagnosis of AIDS is made by a physician using certain clinical criteria.

ACQUIRED IMMUNODEFICIENCY SYNDROME (AIDS)

AIDS is the acronym for Acquired Immunodeficiency Syndrome. The "A" for *acquired* means that the condition is acquired—i.e., the person becomes infected with it. The "ID" for *immunodeficiency,* means that the same as it does in HIV—i.e., the condition affects a person's immune system, which becomes deficient and does not work properly. The "S" for *syndrome* means that the person with AIDS may experience other diseases and infections due to a weakened immune system.

THE RELATIONSHIP BETWEEN HIV AND AIDS

HIV interferes with the normal functioning of the immune system, and its ability to combat infections and disease. The most devastating effect suffered by an HIV-infected individual is the gradual depletion of CD4 cells, which assist in regulating the human immune system. These types of infections are known as "opportunistic" infections because they take the "opportunity" a weakened immune system gives to cause illness.

AIDS is the advanced state of infection caused by HIV. Most people who are HIV-positive are not considered to have AIDS until their immune system becomes so weak it is unable to fight off certain other kinds of infections and illnesses, such as cancer. An HIV-positive person may also be considered to have AIDS if a laboratory test determines that the person's CD4 cell count falls below a certain number, e.g., less than 200. A normal CD4 cell count ranges between 600 to 1,200.

Thus, AIDS is essentially the final stage of the HIV disease, and many members of the scientific and medical community refer to AIDS as HIV disease. Since 1992, scientists have estimated that about half the people with HIV develop AIDS within 10 years after becoming infected.

This time varies greatly from person to person and can depend on many factors, including a person's health status and their health-related behaviors.

SIGNS AND SYMPTOMS OF EARLY HIV INFECTION

Most people who are HIV-positive do not look sick, however, they may exhibit certain symptoms when they first become infected. This period of early infection is known as acute HIV infection. Although symptoms may vary, they may include fever, fatigue, headache, swollen lymph nodes, mouth sores, and skin rash. The symptoms frequently occur in the first few weeks after exposure before antibody test results become positive. If HIV infection is suspected, the patient should receive immediate nucleic acid testing to detect the presence of HIV.

Antiretroviral Therapy

Recent studies have indicated that initiation of antiretroviral therapy during this early period following infection can delay the onset of HIV-related complications and might impact prognosis. The optimal antiretroviral regimen at this time is unknown. According to the CDC, treatment with zidovudine (ZDV) can delay the onset of HIV-related complications, however, most medical experts recommend treatment with two nucleoside reverse transcriptase inhibitors and a protease inhibitor.

HIV testing is discussed more fully in Chapter 4, HIV Testing and Related Issues, of this Almanac.

STATUS OF A CURE

There is presently no known cure for AIDS. There are medical treatments and drug therapies that can slow down the rate at which HIV weakens the immune system. There are other treatments that can prevent or cure some of the illnesses associated with AIDS. As with all other diseases, early detection offers more options for treatment and preventative care. There are many treatments now that can help people with HIV. As a result, many HIV-infected people are living much longer and healthier lives than before.

As set forth below, drug therapy has been effective in prolonging the lives of many HIV-infected persons. Other drugs, known as "prophylactics," have been successful in preventing certain HIV symptoms from developing.

Through constant research efforts, additional drugs are being developed to help make the lives of HIV-infected individuals healthier and longer. People who are HIV-positive need to work closely with their

THE MEDICAL ASPECTS OF HIV/AIDS

doctors to decide when to start treatment and which drugs to take. Some of the more common drug therapies are discussed below.

Combination Therapy

Currently, medicines can slow the growth of the virus or stop it from making copies of itself. Although these drugs don't kill the virus, they keep the amount of virus in the blood low. The amount of virus in the blood is called the viral load, and it can be measured by a test. The lower the viral load, the longer a person can stay healthy and fight off infections.

There are several types of anti-HIV drugs. Each type attacks the virus in its own way. Most people who are getting treated for HIV take 3 or more drugs ("the cocktail"). This form of treatment has been termed drug combination therapy. It also has a longer name: Highly Active Anti-Retroviral Therapy (HAART).

Combination therapy is the most effective treatment for HIV. The "cocktail" include medicines called "protease inhibitors" which are able to reduce HIV to undetectable levels in the bloodstream. Protease Inhibitors block an enzyme crucial to the multiplication of HIV occurring at a late stage of replication. Combined with drugs like AZT, which attack HIV at an earlier stage of replication, the mixture is a powerful treatment.

The HIV "cocktail" medicines have become much easier to take in recent years. Some newer drug combinations package 3 separate medicines into only 1 or 2 pills, taken once a day, with minimal side effects. Still, taking medicine for HIV can be complicated. On one hand, some of the drugs are difficult to take, can cause serious side effects, and don't work for everyone.

Even when a drug does help a particular person, it may become less effective over time or stop working altogether. On the other hand, the drugs help keep HIV under control. Thus, once on medications, patients must work with their doctors to monitor how well the drugs are working, deal with side effects, and decide what to do if the drugs stop working.

Gene Therapy—Stem Cell Delivery

Researchers at Colorado State University discovered a way to deliver HIV-resistant genes into the blood-forming stem cells in a person's bone marrow. The genes then replicate to alter the genetic makeup of the bone marrow cells. The reason researchers have targeted the stem cells is that these cells generate other cells that produce blood.

Thus, if the stem cells are HIV-resistant, the blood cells produced should also be resistant. This would include the CD4 cells that HIV attacks and destroys. This delivery system appears promising, however, its success in treating HIV depends on the development of an effective HIV-resistant gene.

Reduction in Perinatally Acquired AIDS

According to the CDC, one of the most significant changes of the 1990s has been the steep decline in perinatally acquired AIDS. Researchers at the 1996 International AIDS Conference presented studies which reinforced earlier findings that perinatal HIV transmission can be reduced by treating the pregnant mother and newborn with zidovudine (ZDV). Researchers cited a drop in infections in the children who they studied from a 21% infection rate prior to 1994 when the guidelines were introduced, to a 10% infection rate. The recent steep decline in perinatally acquired AIDS has been attributed to the rapid implementation of the ZDV drug therapy to prevent perinatal transmission.

In July 1999, a joint Uganda-U.S. sponsored study released findings concerning another highly effective and purportedly safe drug regimen for preventing transmission of HIV from an infected mother to her newborn. This drug therapy is reportedly more affordable and practical than any other examined to date. The study, sponsored by the National Institute of Allergy and Infectious Diseases (NIAID), demonstrates that a single oral dose of the antiretroviral drug nevirapine (NVP) given to an HIV-infected woman in labor, and another to her baby within three days of birth, reduces the transmission rate by half. If implemented widely in developing countries, this intervention could potentially prevent some 300,000 to 400,000 newborns per year from beginning life infected with HIV.

In addition, there have been improved treatments for HIV-infected children, which delays the onset of AIDS-defining illnesses. The rate of perinatal transmission is expected to continue to decline as a result of more aggressive courses of treatment, and more use of obstetrical procedures, such as elective cesarean sections, that reduce HIV transmission. Infected mothers are also cautioned against breastfeeding their newborns insofar as breast milk may transmit the infection to the baby.

THE RELATIONSHIP BETWEEN HIV AND STDs

STD refers to the category of sexually transmitted diseases that include syphilis, gonorrhea, and herpes. Researchers at the 1996 International AIDS Conference stressed the important link between the treatment of STDs and the reduction in the spread of HIV disease. Researchers cited a Tanzanian study where the aggressive treatment of STDs resulted in a 42% reduction in new HIV infections.

STDs are believed to increase the risk of contracting an HIV infection. For example, herpes and syphilis can cause genital ulcers, and untreated STDs often lead to genital tract inflammation. These conditions make it easier for HIV to enter the body. This preventive treatment appears to be the most promising method of reducing the incidence of new HIV infections presently available.

CHAPTER 4:
HIV TESTING AND RELATED ISSUES

WHO SHOULD BE TESTED?

If you have engaged in any behaviors that place you at risk for acquiring HIV, it is recommended that you get an HIV test. If you can answer "yes" to any of the following questions, you are at above-average risk of HIV.

1. Have you ever had "unprotected" oral, vaginal, or anal sex (sex without a condom or other latex barrier)?

2. Have you ever had sex with someone who was an IV drug user or had HIV?

3. Have you ever had a sexually transmitted disease (STD) such as herpes, chlamydia, gonorrhea, trichomoniasis, or hepatitis?

4. Have you ever had an unplanned pregnancy?

5. Have you ever been sexually assaulted (raped, or forced or talked into having sex when you didn't want to)?

6. Have you ever passed out or forgotten what happened after you were drinking or getting high?

7. Have you ever shared needles or other equipment to inject drugs or pierce the skin, such as tattooing?

8. Have you ever received a blood transfusion? (The risk is very low in the United States, but can vary in other countries.)

9. Did your mother have HIV when you were born, or did she die of AIDS?

An individual who regularly engages in any of the above behaviors is advised to undergo HIV testing every year, and should discuss an HIV testing schedule with his or her health care provider. As of 2006, CDC guidelines recommend that any sexually active person aged 13–64 be tested for HIV every year even if that person is at low risk.

In addition, if you have had sex with someone whose history of drug use and/or sexual partners is unknown to you, or if your partner has had many sexual partners, you are at a greater risk of HIV infection. It is recommended that you and your new partner be tested before engaging in sex.

Further, as set forth below, all women who are pregnant, and any woman who plans on becoming pregnant, should be tested to determine whether she is infected with HIV because there are certain drugs that can be administered during pregnancy that reduce her chance of passing the infection on to the baby.

HOW IS HIV DETECTED?

Most HIV tests are antibody tests that measure the antibodies the body makes against HIV. The antibodies are produced once the virus enters the body, however, the rate at which the immune system of an HIV-infected individual produces these antibodies differs. Thus, there is a "window period" between the time an individual is infected with HIV and the time the body produces enough antibodies that can be detected through testing. During this time period, an HIV-infected person will still get a negative test result.

According to the FDA Center for Biologics and Research (CBER), detectable antibodies usually develop within two to eight weeks. The average is about 22 days. Nevertheless, some people take longer to develop detectable antibodies. Most will develop antibodies within three months following infection, however, in very rare cases, it can take up to six months to develop detectable antibodies to HIV. Thus, if the initial negative HIV test was conducted within the first 3 months after possible exposure, repeat testing should be considered in another three months. The HIV antibodies are detectable in at least 95% of patients within 6 months after infection.

The most common HIV tests use blood to detect HIV infection. Tests using saliva or urine are also available. Some tests take a few days for results, but rapid HIV tests can give results in about 20 minutes. All positive HIV tests must be followed up by another test to confirm the positive result. Results of this confirmatory test can take a few days to a few weeks.

The Enzyme Immunoassay (EIA) Test

The Enzyme Immunoassay (EIA) test is the most common method of testing for the HIV virus. HIV testing may be undertaken using the patient's blood, oral fluid, or urine.

Blood Test

In most cases, the EIA test that uses blood drawn from a vein is the most common screening test utilized to look for antibodies to HIV. A positive—i.e., reactive—EIA must be used with a follow-up test such as the Western blot to make a positive diagnosis.

Oral Fluid Test

The oral fluid test—known as OraSure—involves the use of a probe that looks like a toothbrush. The probe is placed in the patient's mouth between their cheek and gums for about 4 minutes. This is an EIA antibody test similar to the standard blood EIA test discussed above. A follow-up Western Blot using the same oral fluid sample is required.

Urine Test

The use of urine for HIV testing is somewhat less sensitive and accurate than that of the blood and oral fluid tests. This is also an EIA antibody test similar to blood EIA tests and requires a follow-up Western Blot using the same urine sample.

The RNA Test

Another type of test is the RNA test that looks for genetic material of the HIV virus directly. The time between HIV infection and RNA detection is generally 9–11 days. RNA tests are more costly and used less often than antibody tests, although they are used in some parts of the United States. RNA tests can be used in screening the blood supply.

The Rapid HIV Test

Consumers have the option of taking a rapid HIV test, some of which test for both HIV–1 and HIV–2. The rapid HIV test produces results within 20 minutes after the sample is collected.

Both the rapid HIV test and the EIA test described above look for the presence of antibodies to HIV. The rapid HIV test is considered to be just as accurate as the EIA. However, as is true for all screening tests, a reactive rapid HIV test result must be confirmed by a supplemental test before a diagnosis of infection can be given.

Because HIV testing requires interpretation and confirmation, rapid HIV tests are only approved and available in a professional health care setting, such as doctors' offices, clinics and outreach testing sites. The availability of rapid HIV tests, which are more expensive than the standard screening tests, may differ from one place to another.

HOME TEST KITS

Many people concerned with privacy and confidentiality choose to use home testing kits to find out if they are infected with the human immunodeficiency virus (HIV) that causes AIDS. HIV home test kits were first licensed in 1997. Numerous home test kits have since become available, however, the only home test kit presently approved by the Food and Drug Administration (FDA) is marketed under the names Home Access HIV-1 Test System or Home Access Express HIV-1 Test System.

Consumers should be aware that many unapproved home test kits are on the market which falsely claim the test can detect antibodies to HIV in the blood or saliva, and provide results in the home in 15 minutes or less. Some unapproved test kits even claim that the product has been approved by the FDA, however, this is false and the FDA takes action against those parties that sell such unapproved test kits.

The testing procedure using the FDA-approved Home Access System involves pricking one's finger with a special device and placing the drops of blood on a specially treated card. Using a person identification number (PIN), the individual mails the blood sample anonymously to a licensed laboratory for testing. Tests using saliva or urine are also available, but not for "at home" use. The kit tests for the presence of antibodies of the virus known as HIV-1 only. It does not have the ability to test for HIV-2, a less common cause of AIDS.

The PIN is used to obtain the test results, and users are provided with an interpretation of the test results. Users are also offered pre- and post-test, anonymous and confidential counseling through both printed material and telephone interaction.

The FDA-approved Home Access test kit is manufactured by Illinois-based Home Access Health Corporation. The test kit can be purchased at pharmacies, by mail order, or online. To verify that a certain type of HIV test is FDA-approved, consumer may consult the FDA's list of home test kits on the Internet (www.fda.gov/cber/products/testkits.htm) or contact CBER by telephone (800-835-4709) or e-mail (octma@cber.fda.gov).

INFORMED CONSENT

Prior to performing any type of invasive procedure or non-customary treatment, the health care provider is obligated to obtain the patient's informed consent. Thus, informed consent must be obtained before an HIV test is performed, and before any course of HIV drug therapy is initiated, particularly if it is experimental in nature. Some states also require written consent.

In general, informed consent requires that the patient be advised of the risks and benefits of the proposed procedure or treatment, the alternatives to the procedure or treatment, and the risk of not having the procedure performed or treatment undertaken. The informed consent requirement is fulfilled if the patient is advised of the risks and benefits of HIV testing or treatment versus not having the test performed or treatment rendered.

If the health care provider does not obtain such consent, any procedure performed or treatment rendered is deemed unauthorized and the health care provider will be liable to the patient for any negative consequences. In addition, because an individual has an absolute right to prevent an unauthorized contact with his or her person, testing without the patient's consent may be actionable as battery.

A sample Informed Consent to Perform an HIV Test is set forth in Appendix 27.

A patient gives consent to a medical procedure or treatment either by: (1) express consent; or (2) implied consent.

Express Consent

Express consent is obtained either in writing or orally. The health care provider is required to fully disclose all of the known and significant facts relevant to the procedure or treatment, in layperson's language, so that the patient can make an intelligent decision as to whether to go forward with the procedure or treatment.

Implied Consent

Implied consent is obtained, for example, when a patient submits to a *simple* procedure. However, there is no implied consent where the procedure is invasive or non-customary. Implied consent would not be sufficient for a health care provider to proceed with HIV testing or treatment.

Lack of Informed Consent

Lack of informed consent means that the patient did not fully understand what the health care provider was going to do, and was injured as a result of the health care provider's action. Further, the patient claims that if he had known what the health care provider planned to do, the patient would not have consented and, therefore, would have avoided the injury.

Informed Consent and Prescription Drug Therapy

HIV drug therapy treatment involves the administration of many prescription medications. Oftentimes, a patient is prescribed medication without any details given to them about the particular medication. They simply take the often illegibly handwritten prescription to the pharmacy, have it filled, and start taking the drug according to the label's directions. However, patients have the right to know much more about the medicines that they are taking, and should take advantage of those rights.

Most problems associated with prescription drugs occur because the patient did not receive enough information concerning the medicine to use it properly. For example, they are unaware of what side effects to expect, or they improperly mix the medication with a food or drink, or another medication. The improper use of prescription medications can be deadly.

It is important to ask your medical provider every question you may have concerning a medication that is prescribed for you. A patient has the right to be informed about all aspects of their medical treatment, including the risks and benefits of the medicines prescribed; the potential side effects; and the necessity of monitoring the medication's effects. The patient also has the right to know the results of any tests that demonstrate whether or not the medication is working.

MANDATORY TESTING

There have been many attempts to have the government initiate mandatory testing in order to stop the spread of AIDS. These attempts have been met with strong opposition. Proponents for mandatory testing claim that individuals who test positive can take precautionary measures to prevent further spread of HIV. However, opponents of mandatory testing, such as The American Civil Liberties Union (ACLU), have made a number of arguments against mandatory testing, stating that:

1. Testing does not change behavior and cannot stop the spread of the disease.

2. Testing may force people to avoid seeking health care.

3. Testing is undertaken on a mass scale thus there is the probability that many people will either test falsely positive or falsely negative, causing unnecessary suffering and resulting in limited value.

4. Potential discoverability and abuse of the collected data would increase the vulnerability of large numbers of people to discrimination, and infringe on their constitutional right to privacy, as further discussed below.

All states have provisions regarding anonymity and/or confidentiality of HIV testing.

A table of state anonymity/confidentiality HIV testing options is set forth in Appendix 28.

Mandatory Testing of Newborn Infants

The House and Senate have agreed upon a provision, which requires states to conduct mandatory HIV testing of newborns. Obviously, once identified, the drug therapy described in Chapter 2, HIV/AIDS Statistics, can be immediately employed. However, according to the CDC, because HIV antibody crosses the placenta, its presence in a child aged less than 18 months is not diagnostic of HIV infection. Therefore, a definitive determination must be made by laboratory testing.

A sample Informed Consent to Perform an Expedited HIV Test in the Delivery Setting is set forth in Appendix 29.

PARTNERSHIP NOTIFICATION

Partner notification refers to the process of identifying sex and/or needle-sharing partners of individuals infected with HIV or another infectious communicable disease, and advising those partners that they have been exposed to the disease. The rationale behind partner notification is that it allows identification, treatment, and education of individuals who have been exposed to a communicable disease, preventing the spread of the disease and helping people understand how to avoid future infection.

Voluntary partner notification plans encourage an infected individual to notify his or her partners and are viewed as an important component of effective HIV prevention and treatment. However, there has been much criticism of mandatory notification laws. The ACLU has strongly denounced such statutes, stating that available evidence does not justify coercive partner notification but rather demonstrates that mandatory partner notification will not work. They are concerned that mandatory notification will deter people from getting tested in the first place. They further point out that there is no drug therapy that will cure HIV or prevent its transmission, and that because the incubation period is so long, it makes it difficult for patients to identify and locate past partners. Further, there are serious concerns about confidentiality and social stigma attached to the disease.

Nevertheless, because of the development of successful drug therapies that have allowed HIV-infected individuals to live longer and healthier lives—particularly when the treatment is started as soon as the infection has been diagnosed—there has been a movement toward mandatory partner notification.

The Center for Disease Control and Prevention (CDC) has developed guidelines that urge states to formulate voluntary, confidential partner notification services. While some states have followed these guidelines, others have opted to include mandatory notification provisions. In those jurisdictions, an HIV-infected individual who fails to notify their present and past partners may be subject to a fine and/or imprisonment. Some jurisdictions require the health care providers to undertake notification regardless of whether the patient has already done so, and whether or not the patient has consented to the notification.

A table of state statutes concerning HIV partnership notification is set forth in Appendix 30.

NAME-REPORTING REQUIREMENTS

As part of the HIV surveillance initiative, 48 states and the District of Columbia have initiated name-based reporting requirements, and 2 states have code-based reporting requirements. Code-based reporting refers to an HIV surveillance technique where coded identifiers are substituted for names. These codes are used by the state to conduct follow-up activities such as filling in gaps in information on an individual's clinical status.

A table of state HIV reporting requirements is set forth in Appendix 31.

THE HIPAA PRIVACY RULE

Information concerning an individual's medical condition is of interest to a number of entities for a variety of reasons, including insurance carriers, employers, health care providers, government agencies, and law enforcement. All states require AIDS reporting and the majority of states require some reporting for HIV. However, privacy and confidentiality of an individual's medical information is of paramount concern and, without legal safeguards, there is the potential for virtually unlimited access to one's medical records without his or her knowledge or consent.

In enacting the Health Insurance Portability and Accountability Act (HIPAA) Privacy Rule, Congress mandated the establishment of Federal standards for the privacy of individuals' medical records and other personal health information. For example, the Privacy Rule:

1. Gives patients more control over their health information;

2. Sets boundaries on the use and release of health records;

3. Establishes appropriate safeguards that health care providers and others must achieve to protect the privacy of health information;

4. Holds violators accountable, with civil and criminal penalties that can be imposed if they violate patients' privacy rights; and

5. Strikes a balance when public responsibility supports disclosure of some forms of data—for example, to protect public health.

The Privacy Rule also enables patients to make informed choices when seeking care and reimbursement for care based on how personal health information may be used. For example, the Privacy Rule:

1. Enables patients to find out how their information may be used, and about certain disclosures of their information that have been made;

2. Limits the release of information to the minimum reasonably needed for the purpose of the disclosure;

3. Gives patients the right to examine and obtain a copy of their own health records and request corrections; and

4. Empowers individuals to control certain uses and disclosures of their health information.

The Privacy Rule requires the average health care provider or health plan to:

1. Notify patients about their privacy rights and how their information can be used;

2. Adopt and implement privacy procedures for its practice, hospital, or plan;

3. Train employees so that they understand the privacy procedures;

4. Designate an individual to be responsible for seeing that the privacy procedures are adopted and followed; and

5. Secure patient records containing individually identifiable health information so that they are not readily available to those who do not need them.

The HIPAA Compliant Authorization

The HIPAA compliant authorization is a detailed document that gives covered entities permission to use protected health information for specified purposes, which are generally other than treatment, payment, or health care operations, or to disclose protected health information to a third party specified by the individual. A proper authorization must specify a number of elements, including;

1. A description of the protected health information to be used and disclosed;

2. The person authorized to make the use or disclosure;

3. The person to whom the covered entity may make the disclosure;

4. An expiration date; and

5. The purpose for which the information may be used or disclosed.

The Privacy Rule does not require the authorization to be notarized or witnessed.

A sample Authorization for the Release of Health Information Pursuant to HIPAA is set forth in Appendix 32.

Based on the signed authorization, a medical provider may use or disclose a patient's entire medical record provided the authorization describes, among other things, the information to be used or disclosed in a *specific and meaningful fashion*. For example, an authorization would be valid if it authorized the medical provider to use or disclose an "entire medical record" or "complete patient file."

However, an authorization that permits the covered entity to use or disclose "all protected health information" might not be sufficiently specific. This is because protected health information encompasses a wider range of information than that which is typically understood to be included in the "medical record," and individuals are less likely to understand the extent of the information that may be defined as "protected health information."

The authorization remains valid until its expiration date or event, unless effectively revoked in writing by the individual before that date or event. The revocation must be in writing, and is not effective until the covered entity receives it. In addition, a written revocation is not effective with respect to actions a covered entity took in reliance on a valid authorization.

In addition, the Privacy Rule requires the authorization to clearly state the individual's right to revoke, and the process for revocation must be set forth clearly on the authorization itself.

Preemption of State Laws

State laws that are contrary to the Privacy Rule are preempted by the Federal requirements. Nevertheless, a state law may not be preempted by the Privacy Rule if a specific exception applies, as follows:

1. A state law relates to the privacy of individually identifiable health information and is more stringent than the Privacy Rule, i.e., the state law provides greater privacy protections or privacy rights with respect to such information;

2. A state law provides for the reporting of disease or injury, child abuse, birth, or death, or for public health surveillance, investigation, or intervention; or

3. A state law requires certain health plan reporting, such as for management or financial audits. In these circumstances, a covered entity is not required to comply with a contrary provision of the Privacy Rule.

In addition, the Department of Health and Human Services (HHS) may, upon specific request from a state or other entity or person, determine that a provision of state law which is "contrary" to the Federal requirements, and which meets certain additional criteria, will not be preempted by the Federal requirements., e.g., if the state law is necessary for purposes of serving a compelling public health, safety, or welfare need.

HIV TESTING OF PREGNANT WOMEN

The CDC recommends HIV screening of all pregnant women because risk-based testing—i.e., when the health care provider offers an HIV test based on the provider's assessment of the pregnant woman's risk—misses many women who are infected with HIV. HIV testing during pregnancy is important because antiviral therapy can improve the mother's health and greatly lower the chance that an HIV-infected pregnant woman will pass HIV to her infant before, during, or after birth. HIV testing also allows pregnant women to make informed choices that can prevent transmission to their infant. The treatment is most effective for babies when started as early as possible during pregnancy. However, there are still great health benefits to beginning treatment even during labor or shortly after the baby is born.

PREMARITAL HIV TESTING

Presently, there is no state that requires HIV testing in order to obtain a marriage license. A number of states had considered passing such legislation, however, the few that did enact and enforce premarital HIV testing subsequently repealed their laws. Nevertheless, state legislators continue to consider such legislation.

Proponents of mandatory premarital HIV testing argue that identifying infected persons would assist in preventing HIV transmission by alerting the prospective spouse to the risk of exposure, and would further prevent the birth of HIV-infected babies. They also argue that a number of states test for other sexually transmitted diseases, such as syphilis, prior to issuing a license.

Opponents of premarital HIV testing argue that the benefits of such a requirement are few and not cost-effective. Premarital HIV testing is expensive and research has shown that such testing only results in identifying a negligible number of HIV-infected individuals, in large part because individuals seeking marriage licenses constitute a very low-risk population. They also argue that the money spent in operating such a program could be better spent on HIV/AIDS research and treatment and, as an alternative to mandatory testing, funding for AIDS education programs for marriage license applicants.

BLOOD DONATIONS AND BLOOD SUPPLY SAFETY

According to the CDC, the U.S. blood supply is among the safest in the world. Nearly all people infected with HIV through blood transfusions received those transfusions before 1985, the year HIV testing began for all donated blood. U.S. blood donations have been screened for antibodies to HIV since March 1985. Blood and blood products that test positive for HIV are safely discarded and are not used for transfusions. The ELISA test described above has been distributed to blood banks across the nation and has virtually eliminated the likelihood of contracting the HIV virus through blood transfusions.

Currently, the risk of infection with HIV in the United States through receiving a blood transfusion or blood products is extremely low and has become progressively lower, even in geographic areas with high HIV prevalence rates. The FDA Center for Biologics and Research (CBER), is responsible for ensuring the safety of the more than 14 million units of blood and blood components donated by volunteers each year in the United States. The FDA's standards and regulations regarding blood donations and processing help protect the health of both the donor and the recipient.

FDA Safeguards

Some people are concerned that they might get an HIV infection by donating or receiving blood. However, the FDA has set forth stringent safety procedures and standards for the blood industry. The FDA has instituted five layers of overlapping safeguards:

1. Donor Screening—Donors are asked specific and direct questions about their medical history and other factors that may affect the safety of their blood. This preliminary screening eliminates about 90% of ineligible donors, also known as "deferred" donors.

2. Donor Deferral Lists—Blood establishments are required to keep a current list of deferred donors and check all potential donors against that list to prevent the use of blood from deferred donors.

3. Blood Testing—After donation, each unit of donated blood undergoes a series of tests to detect several different infectious disease agents, including hepatitis B; hepatitis C; HIV-1 and HIV-2, which causes AIDS; HTLV-I and HTLV-II, which can cause infections leading to leukemia; and syphilis.

4. Quarantine—Donated blood must be quarantined until it is tested and shown to be free of infectious agents.

5. Problems and Deficiencies—Blood centers must investigate manufacturing problems, correct all deficiencies, and notify the FDA when product deviations occur in distributed products.

If a violation of any one of the above safeguards occurs, the blood product is considered unsuitable for transfusion and is subject to recall.

In addition, FDA scientists are working to produce sensitive donor screening tests to: (1) detect bioterrorist agents in blood donations; and (2) improve blood donor testing kits to detect variable strains of HIV, West Nile virus, hepatitis viruses, and the parasite that causes Chagas disease, a serious and potentially fatal infection. In addition, FDA's Blood Safety Team regularly looks at donor deferral issues to update eligibility requirements when appropriate.

Donor Eligibility

In order to donate blood, the donor must meet certain basic requirements. For example, the blood donor must:

1. Feel well and be able to perform normal activities;

2. Have a blood pressure within normal limits;

3. Have a normal temperature;

4. Be free from acute respiratory diseases;

5. Be at least 16 years old;

6. Have a normal blood hemoglobin level; and

7. Not have donated blood in the last 56 days.

In addition, there are a number of conditions that may make a potential donor temporarily or permanently ineligible to give blood, including:

1. Past use of needles to take drugs that were not prescribed by a doctor;

2. Being a male who has had sexual contact with another male since 1977;

3. Getting a tattoo in the prior year unless performed under sterile conditions; and/or

4. Living in or visiting certain countries during designated periods of time.

Nevertheless, if you are making a donation for your own use prior to surgery, known as an autologous donation, the eligibility rules are less strict.

CHAPTER 5:
ANTI-DISCRIMINATION LEGISLATION

IN GENERAL

In almost all cases, persons infected with HIV are included under existing federal and state statutes, which prohibit discrimination against persons with disabilities. The protection often extends to people who are related in some way to an HIV-infected person. These anti-discrimination statutes typically protect a disabled person provided he or she does not pose a "significant risk" to the health and safety of others. Because research has shown that HIV cannot be transmitted through casual contact, it is unlikely that an infected individual would pose such a significant risk.

Anti-discrimination statutes also typically require employers to make "reasonable accommodations" for disabled persons, which will enable them to do their job. However, an employer is generally not subject to this requirement if it will cause an undue burden.

The primary federal anti-discrimination statutes, which concern individuals infected with HIV/AIDS, are set forth below.

THE REHABILITATION ACT OF 1973

The Rehabilitation Act of 1973 was the most significant legislation protecting the rights of handicapped persons prior to the enactment of the Americans with Disabilities Act of 1990 (ADA). The Rehabilitation Act provides, in part, that "[n]o otherwise qualified individual with handicaps . . . shall, solely by reason of her or his handicap, be excluded from the participation in, be denied the benefits of, or be subject to discrimination under any program or activity receiving Federal financial assistance or under any program or activity conducted by an Executive agency. . ."

Terminology

Handicapped is a term, which has largely been replaced by the term *disabled*, but was in general usage at the time the statute was enacted. A handicapped person under the statute is defined as a person who:

1. Has a physical or mental impairment that substantially limits one or more of such person's major life activities;

2. Has a record of such an impairment; or

3. Is regarded as having such an impairment.

The definition has been interpreted to include HIV-infected individuals.

The term *otherwise qualified* requires that the disabled person:

1. Is able to perform the essential functions of the activity with reasonable accommodation; and

2. Does not create a health or safety risk to others that cannot be eliminated through reasonable accommodation.

The Rehabilitation Act also requires that the act of discrimination occur "solely by reason of handicap." Thus, if mixed motives for the discriminatory act were present, one of which is deemed legitimate by the court, the defendant will generally prevail in an anti-discrimination suit.

The applicability of The Rehabilitation Act of 1973 to education and employment is further discussed below.

THE AMERICANS WITH DISABILITIES ACT OF 1990 (ADA)

The Americans With Disabilities Act (ADA), which was passed by Congress in 1990, is by far the most important piece of legislation prohibiting discrimination against the disabled, including persons infected with HIV. However, the ADA does not preempt any other federal, state or local statutes, which provide equal or greater protection to the disabled.

The ADA applies to discrimination in:

1. Employment;

2. Access to public transportation;

3. Public accommodations; and

4. Telecommunications.

The ADA is applicable to the states and their subdivisions, many public and private employers, and virtually all places of public accommodation. The ADA expands upon the protections provided for in the

Rehabilitation Act of 1973. In fact, the ADA borrows much of the same language used in the Rehabilitation Act.

For example, the ADA's definition of a disabled person is almost identical to that of handicapped persons found in the Rehabilitation Act. It includes those persons:

1. Having a physical or mental impairment that substantially limits one or more major life activities;

2. Having a record of such an impairment; or

3 Regarded as having such an impairment.

The ADA also incorporates the term *qualified individual* giving it the same meaning as the Rehabilitation Act's term, *otherwise qualified individual.*

The ADA has also extended protection to persons who have a "relationship or association" with a disabled person. For example, a family member or friend of an HIV-infected individual is protected under the statute if he or she is subjected to discrimination due to that relationship.

One major difference between the Rehabilitation Act and the ADA is the standard of proof required to show discrimination. As discussed above, under the Rehabilitation Act, the discrimination must be "solely by reason of handicap." The ADA uses the standard of proof applied in Title VII cases, which requires that the plaintiff need only show that the disability was a factor in the discriminatory act.

The applicability of The Americans With Disabilities Act to education and employment is further discussed below.

EDUCATION DISCRIMINATION

A sad outcome of the AIDS epidemic has been the cruel discrimination of schoolchildren who have unfortunately been diagnosed as HIV positive. Young children have become HIV-infected in a number of ways. Babies may become infected from their mothers. This may occur in utero, during the birthing process, or through breastfeeding. Other children are infected by receiving tainted blood or blood products, or in accidents involving exchanges of blood. Still other children, particularly adolescents, are infected in the more commonly known ways, such as through unprotected sexual relations or intravenous drug use. Many of these children now live beyond the age of starting school due to effective drug therapy.

The law has attempted to address the needs of these children in the education process by making sure that they are not subjected to discrimination, and that they receive special services to meet their individual needs. In addition to applicable state and local statutes, there are three important federal statutes that impact HIV/AIDS and the right to an education:

1. The Rehabilitation Act of 1973;

2. The Americans with Disabilities Act of 1990 (ADA); and

3. The Individuals with Disabilities Education Act (IDEA).

Education Discrimination Under the Rehabilitation Act

The Rehabilitation Act prohibits public and private schools that receive federal funding from discriminating against *handicapped* individuals, as defined above. HIV-positive children have been deemed handicapped under the statute, and are thus protected.

A violation of the statute may occur if a child is excluded from school, or segregated from the general school population, *by reason of* the child's handicap. This prohibition applies even if the child has an infectious or contagious illness.

Nevertheless, discrimination does not violate the statute unless the child is *otherwise qualified* or able to participate in school activities. For example, an HIV-infected child may be too fatigued to participate in certain physical fitness activities. In that case, excluding the child from such activities would not violate the statute because the child is not *otherwise qualified* to participate.

If a determination is made that the disabled child is not *otherwise qualified*, there is an affirmative duty upon the school to make reasonable accommodations to compensate for the lack of qualification.

Education Discrimination Under the Americans With Disabilities Act

The Americans With Disabilities Act (ADA) prohibits public schools from discriminating against a qualified individual who is *disabled*, as defined above. HIV-positive children have been deemed disabled under the statute, and are thus protected. A major difference between the ADA and the Rehabilitation Act is that the ADA does not have a federal funding requirement, and does not apply to private schools.

The Individuals With Disabilities Education Act (IDEA)

The IDEA guarantees disabled children the right to a *free appropriate public education*. The IDEA provides for special education programs and related services to address the needs of the disabled student.

The IDEA sets forth a list of disabilities that are covered by the statute. These include:

1. Mental retardation;

2. Hearing, speech and sight impairments;

3. Serious emotional disturbance;

4. Orthopedic impairment; and

5. Other health impaired children.

The statute also covers children with certain learning disabilities that require special education services. An HIV-infected child may have symptoms that fall under the statute's definition. If so, that child is entitled to a *free appropriate public education*, including all of the related services and mandated procedural protections.

EMPLOYMENT DISCRIMINATION

HIV-infected individuals are also protected from discrimination in the workplace on the basis of their HIV status. In addition to applicable state and local statutes, The Rehabilitation Act and The Americans With Disabilities Act also impact HIV/AIDS and discrimination in the workplace.

The ADA applies to any private business or state and local government employer with more than 15 employees. State and/or local laws may cover smaller businesses. In addition, as set forth below, the Rehabilitation Act bans federally funded employers from discriminating against people with disabilities.

Employment Discrimination Under the Rehabilitation Act

The Rehabilitation Act prohibits discrimination against *handicapped persons* in the workplace by federal agencies, including the U.S. Postal Service; businesses which contract with the federal government; and businesses that receive federal funding. The Rehabilitation Act further requires the implementation of affirmative action programs for the employment of handicapped persons.

Under the Rehabilitation Act, discrimination may occur if a person infected with a contagious disease, who is *otherwise qualified*, is terminated. The criteria for determining whether a person is *otherwise qualified* was set forth by the Supreme Court in *School Board of Nassau County v. Arline*, a case involving the termination of a teacher infected with tuberculosis.

The court pointed out that although persons with a contagious disease are covered under the Act, an individual inquiry must be made into the precise nature of the risk involved in the workplace, and whether the employer can make *reasonable accommodations* for the individual that would eliminate or substantially decrease the risk of transmission.

The court set forth four factors to determine whether an employee is *otherwise qualified*, including:

1. The nature of the risk of transmission;

2. The duration of the risk of transmission;

3. The severity of the risk of transmission; and

4. The probabilities the disease will be transmitted.

Under the Rehabilitation Act, the standard of proof required to prove discrimination against one's employer is more strict than that later enacted in the ADA. Under the Rehabilitation Act, an employee is required to prove that their handicap was the sole reason for the discriminatory action. If an employer is able to articulate a nondiscriminatory reason for the adverse action, the employee will not prevail. This is so even if the employer fails to deny the allegations concerning discrimination.

Employment Discrimination Under the Americans With Disabilities Act

Unlike the Rehabilitation Act, the ADA is not limited to federal agencies, contractors or businesses receiving federal funding. Covered workplace entities include employers, employment agencies, labor organizations or joint labor-management committees. Any corporation wholly owned by the United States, an Indian tribe, or a bona fide private membership club is exempt.

Under the ADA, unlike the Rehabilitation Act, an employee does not have to prove that his or her disability was the sole reason for the discriminatory action. The employee need only prove that discrimination was a substantial factor in the employer's decision, where there are mixed motives for the adverse action.

Discrimination is defined as limiting, segregating or classifying a job applicant or employee in a way that adversely affects the opportunities or status of such applicant or employee because of the disability. Further, the ADA applies to virtually all terms, conditions and privileges of employment, including application procedures, hiring, compensation, training, promotion, and termination.

The employee, however, must be deemed *qualified* to be covered by the ADA. This means that he or she must be able to perform the essential functions of the position with or without *reasonable accommodations*.

The ADA provides that an employer's failure to make reasonable accommodations to the known physical or mental limitations of the qualified disabled individual would be deemed discrimination unless the employer can prove that such accommodation would impose an undue hardship on the business, such as creating a significant expense.

For example, due to technical innovations such as the personal computer, modem and fax machine, disabled persons who need to spend time resting at home rather than traveling to and from an office may be able to perform most, if not all, of their work at home. If the disabled person's position is one which would lend itself easily to such a setup, and would not cause an undue burden or expense on the business, the employer may be obligated to make this *reasonable accommodation* instead of terminating the employee.

The ADA further provides that reassignment of the qualified disabled person to another position, other than the one held or desired by that person is not a reasonable accommodation under the law and is thus prohibited.

Nevertheless, if, despite the availability of reasonable accommodations, the employee suffers from symptoms that make it impossible for the individual to function in the position; or poses a direct and significant threat to the health or safety of other individuals in the workplace, terminating the employee would not be a violation of the ADA.

In order to enforce its provisions, the ADA incorporates the enforcement provisions of Title VII of the Civil Rights Act of 1964, as amended. Title VII provides for administrative remedies that must be exhausted before the Equal Employment Opportunity Commission (EEOC) will issue the aggrieved party a "right to sue" letter.

Once a right to sue letter is issued, the claimant is permitted to bring an action in civil court. Prior to that time, the EEOC has jurisdiction for 180 days from the date of the complaint, to investigate and attempt to settle the claim. However, the EEOC has the option of issuing a right to sue letter prior to the expiration of the 180-day limit.

Employment Discrimination Under State and Local Laws

The federal anti-discrimination statutes discussed above are the primary protections afforded an HIV-infected employee who believes he or she has been the subject of discrimination due to his or her disability. However, there are additional considerations concerning employer liability, which should not be overlooked. Many state and local jurisdictions have enacted comprehensive laws protecting HIV-infected persons from discrimination in the workplace.

Virtually all existing state and local laws, which prohibit discrimination against the disabled, have been interpreted to include persons suffering from HIV infection or AIDS. An aggrieved employee always has the federal ADA as a remedy. However, state and local anti-discrimination laws, as well as common-law claims, should not be ignored, and should be joined in an action with the federal claims. In addition, the remedies available under these claims may afford greater damages to the individual, such as the availability of punitive damages, and may be applicable to a broader category of employers.

If a private cause of action is available, the aggrieved individual may be able to forego time-consuming administrative agency procedures and go straight to court. However, one should be aware that in some states, the choice to commence a lawsuit is exclusive, and will bar any administrative review of the claim.

In addition to state and local anti-discrimination laws, the reader should investigate the applicability of related state statutes and common law tort claims, such as breach of contract, intentional or negligent inflection of emotional distress, defamation, and invasion of privacy, etc. A discussion of potential AIDS causes of action are set forth in Chapter 6, HIV/AIDS-Related Litigation.

Constitutional Considerations

The HIV-infected individual has certain rights under the United States Constitution that may be violated. Under the equal protection and due process guarantees of the Constitution, employers are prohibited from treating similarly situated persons in an arbitrary fashion. However, such rights are usually duplicated by the provisions found in anti-discrimination statutes, and disputes are usually decided on that basis.

The Family Medical and Leave Act (FMLA)

In 1993, the Family Medical and Leave Act (FMLA) was enacted to help employees balance their work and family responsibilities by allowing them to take a reasonable amount of unpaid leave for certain family and medical reasons. The basic provisions of the FMLA are set forth below.

Unpaid Job-Protected Leave

The most important provision of the FMLA is the employee's right to unpaid job-protected leave under certain circumstances. The FMLA provides that a *covered employer* must grant an *eligible employee* up to 12 weeks of unpaid, job-protected leave per year.

If the employee has earned or accrued paid leave, such leave may be substituted instead of unpaid leave. If the employee does not elect to substitute paid leave, the employer may require the use of accrued paid leave. In certain cases, FMLA leave may be taken on an intermittent basis—i.e., in segments—rather than all at once, or the employee may work a part-time schedule, known as a reduced leave schedule.

As it pertains to HIV/AIDS, an employee is entitled to take FMLA leave if he or she suffers from a serious health condition that makes the employee unable to perform the functions of his or her job. In addition, an employee may take FMLA leave to take care of an immediate family member who has a serious health condition.

Under the FMLA, a "serious health condition" is generally defined as an illness, injury, impairment, or physical or mental condition that involves: (1) inpatient care in a hospital, hospice, or residential medical care facility; (2) continuing treatment by a health care provider; (3) a period of incapacity or treatment due to a chronic serious health condition; (4) a period of incapacity which is permanent or long-term due to a condition for which treatment may not be effective; and/or (5) any period of absence to receive multiple treatments by a health care provider, including any period of recovery.

Job Protection

Under the FMLA, an employee generally has the right to return to the same position or an equivalent position with equivalent pay, benefits and working conditions at the conclusion of the leave. In fact, taking FMLA leave cannot result in the loss of any employee benefit that accrued prior to the start of the leave.

The employer has the right to 30 days advance notice from the employee that he or she will be taking FMLA leave, if practicable. In addition, the employer may require an employee to submit certification from a health care provider to substantiate that the leave is due to the serious health condition of the employee or the employee's immediate family member. Failure to comply with these requirements may result in a delay in the start of FMLA leave.

The employer may also require that an employee present a certification of fitness to return to work when the absence was caused by the employee's own serious health condition. The employer may delay restoring the employee to employment if the employee does not present such a certificate relating to the health condition that caused their absence.

If an employee's rights under the FMLA are violated by his or her employer, the employee may file a complaint against the employer with the Secretary of Labor; or file a private lawsuit against the employer. If it is shown that the employer violated one or more provisions of the

FMLA, the employee may receive the wages, employment benefits, or other compensation that was denied or lost to the employee due to the violation.

The FMLA and Anti-Discrimination Laws

Nothing in the FMLA modifies or affects any Federal or State law prohibiting discrimination on the basis of race, religion, color, national origin, sex, age, or disability, such as the Americans with Disabilities Act of 1990 (ADA), or Title VII of the Civil Rights Act of 1964. Thus, for example, the leave provisions of the FMLA are wholly distinct from the reasonable accommodation obligations of employers covered under the ADA, as discussed above.

The purpose of the FMLA is to make leave available to eligible employees and employers within its coverage, and not to limit already existing rights and protection. An employer must therefore provide leave under whichever statutory provision provides the greater rights to employees.

When an employer violates both the FMLA and another anti-discrimination law, an employee may be able to recover under either or both statutes, although double relief may not be awarded for the same loss.

CHAPTER 6:
HIV/AIDS-RELATED LITIGATION

IN GENERAL

A number of legal issues surround HIV/AIDS. Potential areas of litigation are discussed below.

THE CRIMINAL TRANSMISSION OF HIV

Since the emergence of HIV and AIDS, society and the courts have become increasingly concerned with the possibility of HIV transmission during sexual relations and as a result of sexual assault or abuse. As further discussed below, many states have enacted criminal statutes, which address these issues.

Elements and Defenses

A key element of a crime involving HIV transmission is intent—i.e., whether or not the HIV-infected individual was aware that they were infected with the virus. Because an individual may have the virus without any symptoms, they may not be aware that they were infected and thus they could not have formed the requisite intent to commit the crime of transmitting the virus.

Where an HIV-infected individual sexually assaults his or her victim, he or she may be subject to an additional attempted murder charge, depending on the jurisdiction. The particular part of the offender's body that was responsible for transmitting the virus—e.g., the mouth or penis, etc.—is considered the "deadly weapon" in such prosecutions. Offenders who know they are infected and engage in sexual relations without the knowledge or consent of their partner may be subject to a criminal assault or reckless endangerment charge.

Some courts have held that a defendant's knowledge of their positive HIV status at the time they engaged in the sexual act constitutes an aggravating circumstance, which may subject the defendant to an enhanced sentence, and can be raised as a reason for departing from otherwise applicable sentencing guidelines.

Many statutes have been amended to permit sexual relations between individuals where the non-infected partner has knowledge of the other partner's HIV status, and, nevertheless, consents to sexual relations with that person. Generally, consent to exposure is an affirmative defense set forth in most statutes.

The South Carolina statute is representative of statutes proscribing the criminal transmission of HIV:

S.C. Code Ann. § 44-29-145

Penalty for exposing others to Human Immunodeficiency Virus:

It is unlawful for a person who knows that he is infected with Human Immunodeficiency Virus (HIV) to:

(1) knowingly engage in sexual intercourse, vaginal, anal, or oral, with another person without first informing that person of his HIV infection;

(2) knowingly commit an act of prostitution with another person;

(3) knowingly sell or donate blood, blood products, semen, tissue, organs, or other bodily fluids;

(4) forcibly engage in sexual intercourse, vaginal, anal, or oral, without the consent of the other person, including one's legal spouse; or

(5) knowingly share with another person a hypodermic needle, syringe, or both, for the introduction of drugs or any other substance into, or for the withdrawal of blood or body fluids from the other person's body without first informing that person that the needle, syringe, or both, has been used by someone infected with HIV.

A person who violates this section is guilty of a felony and, upon conviction, must be fined not more than five thousand dollars or imprisoned for not more than ten years.

A table of state statutes concerning the criminal transmission of HIV/ AIDS is set forth in Appendix 33.

Mandatory Testing of Sexual Assault Defendants

There has been much controversy over whether or not a defendant in a sexual assault case can be compelled to undergo HIV testing, particularly prior to conviction for the sexual assault. Obviously, the sexual assault victim is concerned over whether they have been exposed to the virus, and wants the defendant tested. However, opponents of involuntary testing argue that testing will not prove that the infection was transmitted to the victim, and because of the lag time between exposure and positive testing, it does not provide the victim with any reassurance that they were not exposed. Thus, the victim must still deal with the anxiety of wondering whether they were infected, and whether they are capable of infecting others.

Nevertheless, proponents of compulsory testing argue that there is some psychological benefit to the victim where the defendant tests negative, even if this does not guarantee there was no exposure. Further, if the defendant tests positive, the victim will be able to timely avail himself or herself to rapidly developing prophylactic treatment of HIV.

In jurisdictions, which do not provide any statutory basis for compelling a defendant to undergo an HIV blood test, such a concession may be made as part of any plea bargain arrangement offered by the prosecution.

Disclosure of Test Results

There is also concern over the disclosure of the defendant's private medical record. The extent to which such records can be disclosed varies among the states. Federal law provides that disclosure of the test results can only be given to the victim, the victim's parents or guardians, and the defendant. The victim, in turn, can disclose the results to his or her medical providers, family members and any sexual partner(s) the victim may have had since the attack.

Prisoners and convicted offenders have a constitutional right of privacy that protects them from unwarranted disclosure of their HIV status even if they are subjected to mandatory testing. Thus, where a defendant has not yet been convicted of the crime, there must be adequate safeguards in place to guarantee the confidentiality of the defendant's medical records.

Sexual Abuse of Children

According to the CDC, the identification of sexually transmissible disease in children beyond the neonatal period suggests sexual abuse, with some limited exceptions. Thus, the possibility of sexual abuse should be considered if no obvious risk factor for infection can be identified.

INTENTIONAL TORT CAUSES OF ACTION

An intentional tort refers to a tortious—i.e. a "wrongful"—act perpetrated by one who intends to do that which the law has declared wrong, as contrasted with negligence in which the tortfeasor fails to exercise that degree of care in doing what is otherwise permissible. Unlike criminal actions, which are brought on behalf of the state by the District Attorney, the intentional tort causes of action are civil cases brought by the plaintiff against the responsible party. Potential intentional tort claims in HIV/AIDS litigation may include:

Patient Abandonment

The intentional tort of abandonment may arise in the context of the physician/patient relationship. For example, once a physician undertakes to treat a patient, he or she cannot unilaterally terminate the relationship. The only circumstances under which the physician/patient contract can be terminated are: (1) if the patient terminates the relationship; (2) if there is termination by mutual agreement; (3) if the physician becomes incapacitated; (4) if the patient's illness terminates; or (5) if the treatment sought is successful.

Therefore, if a physician begins treatment of a patient, and during the course of that treatment learns that the patient is HIV-infected, the physician would be liable for abandonment if he or she attempts to terminate the relationship without first obtaining the consent of the patient. If a physician is concerned about exposure to HIV, he or she may require the patient to be tested prior to accepting the patient into treatment.

Battery

Battery is defined as the intentional touching of another without his or her consent. A health care provider may be liable for battery if he or she fails to obtain the consent of the patient prior to undertaking treatment. Informed consent requires that a patient be apprised of the nature and risks of a medical procedure before the physician can validly claim exemption from liability for battery, or from responsibility for medical complications.

Defamation

Defamation is defined as the publication of an injurious statement about the reputation of another. An individual may be liable for defamation if, for example, he or she spreads false information concerning the positive HIV status of another. If the information concerning a positive HIV status is true, defamation would not apply.

Invasion of Privacy

If defamation does not apply, there may be a related cause of action for invasion of privacy. For example, invasion of privacy may apply if there is public disclosure of private facts to a reasonable person, which disclosure is highly offensive, and where there is no legitimate public interest in such disclosure.

Intentional Infliction of Emotional Distress

A cause of action for intentional infliction of emotional distress could arise, for example, if an HIV-infected individual knowingly exposes another person to the disease without forewarning that person that he or she was infected.

Fraud

If intentional infliction of emotional distress does not apply, there may be a related cause of action for fraud. For example, fraud may apply if the HIV-infected individual knowingly and falsely represents that he or she is not infected, with the intention of inducing the plaintiff to act, e.g. engage in sexual relations, and the victim relies on the misrepresentation, to his or her detriment.

NEGLIGENCE

Negligence is defined as the failure to exercise that degree of care which a reasonable person would exercise given the same circumstances. A cause of action for negligence may arise in the context of tainted blood litigation.

For example, if a blood supplier negligently fails to perform the HIV antibody test on donated blood prior to transporting it to the hospital for use, and the blood turns out to be HIV-positive, the blood supplier may be found liable if the recipient of the blood is thereby infected.

MEDICAL RECORDS PRIVACY VIOLATIONS

As set forth in Chapter 4, HIV Testing and Related Issues, the HIPAA Privacy Rule was enacted to protect the privacy of an individual's medical records and other personal health information. Under the Act, if you believe your privacy rights have been violated, and that a medical provider is not complying with a requirement of the Privacy rule, you may file a written complaint with the Office of Civil Rights (OCR). The OCR has authority to receive and investigate complaints against covered entities related to the Privacy Rule. Complaints to the OCR must:

1. Be filed in writing, either on paper or electronically;

2. Name the entity that is the subject of the complaint and describe the acts or omissions believed to be in violation of the applicable requirements of the Privacy Rule; and

3. Be filed within 180 days of when you knew that the act or omission complained of occurred. The OCR may extend the 180-day period if you can show "good cause."

Anyone can file written complaints with OCR by mail, fax, or email. The complaint can be submitted in any written format, but should include the following information:

1. Your name, full address, home and work telephone numbers, and email address.

2. If you are filing a complaint on someone's behalf, provide the name of the person on whose behalf you are filing.

3. The name, full address and phone of the person, agency or organization you believe violated your health information privacy rights or committed another violation of the Privacy Rule.

4. Briefly describe what happened, e.g., how, why, and when you believe your health information privacy rights were violated, or the Privacy Rule was otherwise violated.

The OCR has ten regional offices, and each regional office covers certain states. You should send your complaint to the appropriate OCR Regional Office, based on the region where the alleged violation took place. Complaints should be sent to the attention off the appropriate OCR Regional Manager. Assistance in filing a complaint may be obtained by calling the OCR at 1-800-369-1019.

Individuals also have a right to file a complaint directly with the covered entity, and should refer to the covered entity's notice of privacy practices for more information about how to file a complaint.

CHAPTER 7:
HEALTH CARE AND INSURANCE ISSUES

HEALTH CARE ISSUES

There is growing concern over both the treatment of HIV-infected patients by uninfected health care workers, and the treatment of uninfected patients by HIV-infected health care workers. A number of legal issues have arisen from these scenarios, as further discussed below.

Patient Abandonment and Refusal to Treat

As set forth in Chapter 6, HIV/AIDS-Related Litigation, a physician who begins treatment of a patient cannot unilaterally decide to stop treating the patient. If so, the physician may be liable to the patient for the intentional tort of abandonment. Under the common law, a private physician is free to refuse a patient provided treatment has not yet begun. Nevertheless, because the advent of AIDS has so paralyzed the nation, including health care providers, availability of adequate treatment of this condition has come under scrutiny.

The American Medical Association, as well as certain state licensing boards, has set forth ethical guidelines that provide that physicians who are able to treat an HIV-infected person should do so. Further, certain statutes prohibiting discrimination against the disabled—including HIV/AIDS patients—also limit the physician's right to refuse to treat such individuals. These restrictions on the right to refuse a patient have also been made applicable to private hospitals under state and federal anti-discrimination statutes.

Duty to Protect Uninfected Patients

In addition, the courts have held that health care providers, including hospitals, have a duty to protect uninfected patients from contracting HIV from other patients or infected health care providers. It is not likely that the virus would be transmitted between patients who only have casual contact with each other. It is more likely that an uninfected patient may contract HIV from the health care provider, particularly if invasive-type procedures are being performed, e.g. surgery.

Some jurisdictions require health care providers to disclose their HIV status to patients as part of the informed consent requirement. Nevertheless, a health care provider is prohibited from unnecessarily disclosing the HIV status of a patient. If so, the health care provider may be liable for violation of the individual's right to privacy, and the disclosure may be deemed a breach of confidentiality.

The Needlestick Safety and Prevention Act

The mission of the Occupational Safety and Health Administration (OSHA) is to set standards and enforce rules and regulations designed to prevent such injuries and protect the health of America's workers. Employers are required to comply with these standards, rules and regulations.

In 1991, the Occupational Safety and Health Administration (OSHA) released its bloodborne pathogens standard, intended to protect millions of workers across the nation from workplace exposure to HIV and hepatitis. This standard covers employees exposed to blood and other infectious materials, including but not limited to employees in hospitals, health care facilities, nursing homes, and research laboratories.

Although the bloodborne pathogens standard significantly reduced the risk that workers will contract a bloodborne disease in the course of their work, occupational exposure to bloodborne pathogens from accidental needlesticks and sharps injuries in health care settings continued to be a serious problem.

There has been much concern among health care workers about needle stick injuries involving inappropriately discarded needles. Needlestick injuries can transfer blood and blood-borne pathogens, and can lead to hepatitis B, hepatitis C and Human Immunodeficiency Virus (HIV), the virus that causes AIDS.

Every year, health care workers suffer between 600,000 and one million injuries from conventional needles and sharps annually. Approximately 16,000 of these needlestick injuries each year result in HIV exposure. In addition, there are over 54 documented cases of health care workers with occupationally acquired HIV and at least 133 cases of possible transmissions of HIV. Further, it is estimated that at least 1,000 health care workers contract serious infections annually from needlestick and sharps injuries.

In 2000, in response to this serious problem, Congress enacted The Needlestick Safety and Prevention Act, and OSHA revised its blood-borne pathogens standard. Under the revised standard, employers are required to select safer needle devices and involve employees in identifying and choosing those devices. The updated standard also requires employers to maintain a log of injuries from contaminated sharps.

The text of the Needlestick Safety and Prevention Act is set forth in Appendix 34.

INSURANCE ISSUES

Although the insurance industry is not covered by the Americans with Disabilities Act (ADA), Congress has nevertheless stated that insurers will not be permitted to engage in practices that evade the purposes of the ADA. Some of the important concerns relating to both health and life insurance and the rights of the HIV-infected person are set forth below.

Health Insurance

The AIDS epidemic has caused an extraordinary burden on the health care system and, in turn, the health insurance business. Insurance companies have attempted to shield themselves from catastrophic losses by requiring applicants to undergo HIV testing. However, such requirements have been challenged with contrary results depending on the jurisdiction. Some jurisdictions have enacted legislation specifically prohibiting HIV testing and/or application questions designed to determine if the applicant is a member of a high-risk group.

Some jurisdictions have held that such requirements are nondiscriminatory and, in fact, sound insurance underwriting policies, particularly when underwriting a policy for an individual. The courts have permitted insurers to subject the individual applicant to more stringent requirements.

Nevertheless, when the policy in question is a large group policy, the courts have generally held that an HIV testing requirement is of "less certain validity" because the insurers are assessing risks characteristic of a group rather than a particular individual.

The Health Insurance Portability and Accountability Act (HIPAA)

The Health Insurance Portability and Accountability Act of 1996 (HIPAA) was enacted to address some of the problems facing people who are infected with HIV/AIDS and need health care coverage.

Under HIPAA, exclusions for pre-existing conditions are limited, and group health plans are prohibited from denying health care coverage based on the past or present health condition of the insured's family member. In addition, HIPAA gives those who are losing their group health coverage additional options for obtaining individual coverage, and guarantees certain small employers and individuals who lose job-related coverage the right to purchase individual health insurance.

The Family Medical and Leave Act (FMLA)

The Family Medical and Leave Act (FMLA) protects the employee's right to have their health benefits maintained while on leave as if the employee had continued to work instead of taking the leave. In addition, the employer must continue to pay whatever share of the employee's health care premium the employer was paying prior to the employee's leave period.

If an employee was paying all or part of the premium payments prior to taking leave, the employee must continue to pay his or her share during their leave period. The employer may recover its share only if the employee does not return to work for a reason other than the serious health condition of the employee or the employee's immediate family member, or another reason beyond the employee's control.

The Consolidated Omnibus Budget Reconciliation Act (COBRA)

The FMLA discussed above protects the employee's rights to health benefits while on leave from their employment. The Consolidated Omnibus Budget Reconciliation Act (COBRA) allows employees to continue their health insurance coverage at their own expense for a certain period of time after their employment has ended, provided there is a *qualifying event*. Generally, if an employee must stop working due to health reasons, the period of time for which benefits may be extended ranges from 18 to 36 months.

In general, the benefits available under COBRA are the same as those extended under the original insurance coverage, and may include medical care, including doctor visits; inpatient and outpatient hospital care; surgical care; prescription drugs; and vision and dental care.

Qualifying Events

Qualifying events and the corresponding coverage period include:

1. Termination of employment—18 months;

2. Disability—18 to 29 months;

3. Reduction of work hours with loss of benefits—18 months;

4. Death of a covered employee—Indefinitely for the eligible spouse, and until age 23 for dependent children; or

5. Divorce/legal separation from the covered employee—36 months.

Once it is determined that an employee is entitled to COBRA benefits, the employer is required to provide the employee with notice of his or her rights to continue coverage. The employee must reply within a certain time period, e.g., 60 days, to accept coverage.

Life Insurance

Employees are not entitled to continuation of life insurance coverage such as that provided for medical coverage under COBRA. Underwriters of life insurance policies are similarly concerned with the HIV status of applicants. However, the impact on the life insurance industry is much less than the burden on the health insurance industry due to a number of factors:

1. There is an increased lifespan of HIV-infected individuals due to advances in drug treatment;

2. The largest number of victims thus far have been among groups which are the least likely to purchase life insurance, e.g. minorities;

3. The availability of HIV testing during the application process; and

4. Established insurance principles available to the insurer which will void a life insurance policy under certain conditions, e.g. if there has been material misrepresentation during the application process. For example, if an HIV-infected person denies having certain enumerated medical conditions on their application, when in fact he or she does suffer from such conditions, the life insurance policy would generally be unenforceable and the insurer would not have to pay any benefits.

CHAPTER 8:
HIV/AIDS IN THE MILITARY AND CORRECTIONAL SETTINGS

HIV/AIDS IN THE UNITED STATES MILITARY

The United States Armed Forces are generally exempt from the anti-discrimination statutes set forth in Chapter 5, Anti-Discrimination Legislation. The U.S. Supreme Court has made it clear that constitutional protections that govern civilians are not necessarily applicable to service members.

In 1985, the Secretary of Defense issued a comprehensive AIDS policy, requiring mandatory testing for HIV antibodies by all recruits, active duty personnel and service academy students. The Department of Defense (DOD) policy, as revised in 1987, provides that recruits who test positive for HIV are not eligible for military service. However, the DOD policy explicitly provides that information concerning the positive HIV status of a service member could not be used to support any adverse personnel action against the member, including involuntary separation.

The Dornan Amendment

In February 1996, President Clinton signed into law the military budget bill. Included in the bill was a provision sponsored by Congressman Robert Dornan (R-CA) requiring automatic discharge of HIV-positive service members (The Dornan Amendment). Although President Clinton stated that he considered this provision to be unconstitutional, he failed to veto the bill.

The American Civil Liberties Union (ACLU) has announced its campaign to have this provision repealed. There has also been bi-partisan sponsorship for legislation, which will repeal the discharge requirement (HR 2959). If unsuccessful, the ACLU has stated its intention to challenge the provision in court, supported by other AIDS advocacy organizations.

The Dornan Amendment essentially repeals existing military law, which treats all service members suffering from a serious medical condition equally (10 U.S.C. 1177). The Dornan Amendment isolates HIV-infected service members from other groups suffering from serious medical conditions, and requires their immediate dismissal. Discharge is required regardless of whether they are able to perform their duties, and whether they are symptomatic or asymptomatic.

Conflict Between the Dornan Amendment and Existing DOD Policy

As stated above, the existing DOD policy did not discriminate between HIV-infected service members and others suffering from serious illness. The DOD policy basically provided that service members who test positive for HIV would be separated from the service only upon a medical evaluation demonstrating that they were unfit for duty. This is the same procedure followed in all cases where a service member is suffering from a serious medical condition.

The DOD policy is fair and nondiscriminatory because the main criteria for separation is whether or not the service member is fit for duty. It is a fact that many HIV-infected service members, as well as service members suffering from other serious illnesses, are exceptionally productive individuals, and able to meet the physical fitness requirements of the military.

Constitutional Considerations

On its face, the Dornan Amendment appears to violate the equal protection guarantee of the Constitution, which requires that all persons similarly situated be treated similarly under the law. As stated above, HIV-infected service members are subject to immediate dismissal whereas service members with other serious medical conditions, such as heart disease, tuberculosis or cancer, are not.

Although the argument is made that the purpose of such a requirement is the preservation of military readiness, the equal protection guarantee requires that discrimination between similarly situated individuals be rationally related to a legitimate government purpose.

Thus, it is unlikely that such a purpose can be articulated for discharging a productive HIV-infected service member over a productive service member afflicted with another serious condition. One such purpose that has been cited is the potential impact of HIV transmission on the battlefield, e.g., by emergency transfusions. However, instead of summarily discharging such persons, a better alternative may be to assign them to positions, which would not require such intimate contact.

Prosecution for Unprotected Sex by an HIV-Infected Service Member

The United States Military Court of Appeals has taken the position that an HIV-infected service member who engages in unprotected sex is guilty of an aggravated assault. In such a case, the prosecution does not have to prove that the service member specifically intended to transmit the virus to their partner. The prosecution need only prove general intent, i.e., that the service member intended to have unprotected sexual intercourse with knowledge that he or she was HIV-infected. Further, the partner's consent to sexual relations is not a defense because the consent is only to having sexual relations, not consent to take the risk of being infected.

HIV/AIDS IN THE CORRECTIONAL SETTING

The prison system has been critically affected by the AIDS epidemic. This is because individuals who fall into high-risk groups, such as prostitutes and intravenous drug users, pass through the system on a regular basis. Injection drug use is the leading risk factor for HIV/AIDS in prisons and jails throughout the country, and one-quarter of prisoners have used needles to inject drugs. Nearly half of those prisoners who use illegal drugs have shared needles.

In addition, homosexual activity within the prison setting is not uncommon. Such activity, which is not always consensual, is a known route of HIV transmission. Another method of potential transmission is the practice of tattooing, which is often performed under less than hygienic conditions.

Statistics

According to the most recent report released in September 2007 by the U.S. Department of Justice, Bureau of Justice Statistics, 20,888 state inmates and 1,592 federal inmates were infected with HIV or had confirmed AIDS by the end of 2005. This was a total of 22,480 HIV/AIDS in state and federal prisons, a slight decrease from 22,936 inmates in 2004.

Half of the HIV/AIDS cases were in the South, one-third in the Northeast, and one-tenth in both the Midwest and West. The Northeast reported the highest percentage of HIV/AIDS cases. Three states—New York, Florida and Texas—maintained almost half of all of the HIV/AIDS cases in state prisons.

A table setting forth the number of HIV/AIDS cases in state and federal prisons (Year End 2005) is set forth in Appendix 35.

According to gender, 18,953 males were HIV-infected or confirmed with AIDS, compared to 1,935 female prisoners. Five states—New Hampshire,

North Dakota, West Virginia, Hawaii and Montana—had no female HIV/AIDS cases.

During 2005, an estimated 176 state inmates died from AIDS-related causes, accounting for nearly 1 in 20 deaths reported in state prisons. New York reported the largest number of AIDS-related deaths, followed by Florida and California. The Northeast reported the highest number of AIDS-related deaths. Among federal inmates, there were 27 AIDS-related deaths in 2005.

According to age, older inmates were more likely to die from AIDS-related causes than persons in the same age group in the general population. In 2005, inmates ages 35–44 were almost twice as likely to die from AIDS-related causes. Among inmates ages 45–54, state inmates were more than twice as likely as those in the general population to die from AIDS-related causes.

Rights of the HIV-Infected Prisoner

When institutionalizing an HIV-infected individual, the rights of the individual versus the rights of the general prison population must be considered. It is undisputed that the HIV-infected prisoner has the right to adequate medical treatment. The individual also has a qualified right to access prison facilities and participate in prison programs. In some cases, prisoners have been denied access to certain facilities and programs, e.g. conjugal visit programs. However, in order to withstand judicial scrutiny, such denials must be justifiable taking into consideration the totality of the circumstances.

For example, courts have upheld the segregation of HIV-infected prisoners from the general prison population even though, as a practical matter, this may deny the prisoner access to certain programs, such as recreational activities. The courts generally reason that the risk to the population and the need to maintain security and order in the prison outweigh the individual's interest, and often defer to the judgment of prison officials.

Regulations promulgated by The United States Bureau of Prisons provide that HIV-infected prisoners may not be segregated unless they pose a danger to others. Nevertheless, if an HIV-infected prisoner is segregated, the living conditions under which he or she is placed will be subject to judicial scrutiny.

Testing Protocol

In general, the United States Bureau of Prisons (BOP) policy on testing prisoners for the presence of HIV antibodies provides for random testing of new inmates; random sample testing of the general population;

testing of prisoners who are symptomatic of HIV or otherwise chronically ill; and suggests testing of prisoners who are in high-risk categories. Some jurisdictions routinely test all prisoners.

The BOP criteria for HIV testing for all inmates, regardless of sentencing of duration of stay, includes:

1. Signs or symptoms of acute HIV infection;

2. Sign or symptoms of HIV-related condition;

3. Pregnancy;

4. Recent HIV exposure;

5. Active tuberculosis;

6. Positive tuberculin skin test; or

7. When otherwise clinically indicated.

HIV testing is also undertaken for sentenced inmates (6 months or greater) with the following risk factors:

1. Injected illegal drugs and shared equipment;

2. Males who have sex with other males;

3. Unprotected intercourse with more than one sex partner;

4. History of gonorrhea or syphilis;

5. Inmate from a high-risk country (e.g., Sub-Saharan Africa/West Africa);

6. Received blood products between 1977 and 1985;

7. Hemophilia;

8. Percutaneous exposure to blood; or

9. Upon request of the inmate.

HIV testing of sentenced inmates with HIV risk factors is mandatory BOP policy and federal law. Constitutional challenges to testing have been unsuccessful. The courts have routinely applied an interest balance approach, and have found that the interests of the prison in treating and preventing the virus outweigh the individual prisoner's interests, e.g. right to privacy.

Nevertheless, the unnecessary disclosure of a prisoners' HIV test results to anyone, other than those who have a medical need to be informed, has been held to violate an individual's constitutional right to privacy.

Sentencing Considerations

In many cases, HIV-infected defendants are given lenient sentences, or not prosecuted at all. The defendant's HIV status may also be used as a reason for the Court to depart from otherwise mandatory sentencing guidelines. These actions are sometimes motivated by sympathy, however, it is also true that many penal institutions simply do not want to undertake the cost and difficulties of incarcerating and caring for an HIV-infected prisoner.

Most jurisdictions also have what is called a *Compassionate Release* provision. When a sentenced inmate is terminally ill, and has less than one year of life expectancy remaining, some Courts may commute the sentence to time served, probation, parole, or house arrest.

National Commission on Correctional Health Care

The National Commission on Correctional Health Care (NCCHC) is the largest nationwide educational gathering of physicians, nurses, dentists, psychiatrists, psychologists, other health care professionals, administrators, attorneys, and others working in prisons, jails, juvenile confinement, and detention facilities.

The mission of the NCCHC is to improve the quality of health care in jails, prisons and juvenile confinement facilities. Participants in the Commission meet to discuss correctional health issues and developments in the management and treatment of HIV in the correctional setting.

Contact information for the NCCHC is as follows:

National Commission on Correctional Health Care (NCCHC)

1145 W. Diversey Parkway

Chicago, IL 60614]

Telephone: 773-880-1460

Fax: 773-880-2424

E-mail: info@ncchc.org

Website: http://www.ncchc.org/

APPENDIX 1:
HIV/AIDS RESOURCE DIRECTORY

ORGANIZATION	SERVICES PROVIDED	TELEPHONE	E-MAIL	WEBSITE
ACLU Aids Project	Undertakes litigation, monitors legislation and engages in educational efforts affecting the rights of persons with HIV/AIDS	N/A	N/A	www.aclu.org
Advocates For Youth	Creates programs and promotes policies to help young people make informed and responsible decisions about their sexual health	202-419-3420	information@ advocatesforyouth.org	www.advocatesforyouth. org
AIDS Action	Dedicated to shaping federal policy for people living with HIV/AIDS	202-530-8030	webmaster@aidsaction. org	www.aidsaction.org
AIDS Clinical Trial Information Services	Provides access to information on federally and privately funded clinical trials for adults and children	1-800-TRIALS-A	actis@actis.org	www.actis.org

ORGANIZATION	SERVICES PROVIDED	TELEPHONE	E-MAIL	WEBSITE
AIDS Education Training Centers (AETC)	Provides training and education concerning AIDS	404-727-1513	seatec@emory.edu	www.seatec.emory.edu
AIDS Housing Corporation	Facilitates the creation of housing programs for people living with HIV disease and AIDS	617-927-0088	N/A	www.ahc.org
AIDS Information Global Information System (AEGIS)	AIDS information global information service	949-248-5843	admin@aegis.org	www.aegis.com
AIDS In Prison Project	Information resources for HIV-infected prisoners	1-800-344-3314	info@osborneny.org	www.osborneny.org
AIDS Medicine & Miracles	Promotes the well-being of people confronting AIDS through creative educational programs that address the mind, body, and spirit	415-252-7111	amm@aidsmedicineandmiracles.org	www.csd.net/~amm/mission.php
AIDS National Interfaith Network	Assists AIDS ministries to share resources and provides a public policy presence in Washington representing the faith community	202-842-0010	N/A	www.thebody.com/anin/aninpage.html
AIDS Policy Center for Children, Youth and Families	Serves the public policy concerns of parents, families and young people living with and at risk for HIV/AIDS	202-785-3564	apcyf@aol.com	www.commondreams.org

ORGANIZATION	SERVICES PROVIDED	TELEPHONE	E-MAIL	WEBSITE
AIDS Treatment News	Reports on experimental and standard AIDS treatments	1-800-873-2812	aidsnews@aidsnews.org	www.aidsnews.org
Alternative Medicine Homepage	Referrals to alternative HIV/AIDS medicine resources	N/A	N/A	www.pitt.edu/~cbw/hiv.html
American Bar Association AIDS Coordination Project	Provides assistance to individuals seeking information on legal referral programs and sources of legal information related to HIV/AIDS	202-662-1025	N/A	www.abanet.org/AIDS
American Foundation for AIDS Research (AMFAR)	Supports AIDS research, prevention and advocacy of sound AIDS-related policies	212-806-1600	N/A	www.amfar.org
American Public Health Association	Identifies challenges for public health through its HIV/AIDS Special Primary Interest Group	202-777-2742	comments@apha.org	www.apha.org
American Red Cross	Prepares and certifies instructors to deliver HIV/AIDS prevention education	1-800-REDCROSS	N/A	www.redcross.org
American Social Health Association	Operates the CDC National AIDS Hotline and provides free literature and referrals	919-361-8400	info@ashastd.org	www.ashastd.org
Ark of Refuge, Inc.	Promotes the Harlem Week of Prayer for the Healing of AIDS	415-861-6130	arkinfo@pacbell.net	www.arkofrefuge.org
Asian & Pacific Islanders American Health Forum	National advocacy organization dedicated to promoting policy, program and research efforts	415-954-9988	hr@apiahf.org	www.apiahf.org

ORGANIZATION	SERVICES PROVIDED	TELEPHONE	E-MAIL	WEBSITE
Association of Maternal and Child Health Programs	Assists state Title V programs in reducing perinatal HIV transmission	202-775-0436	N/A	www.amchp.org
Association of Nutrition Services	Assists HIV nutrition providers through technical assistance and advocacy, and provides referrals for individuals seeking local resources	202-737-1011	fabdale@ansanutrition. org	www.aidsnutrition.org
Balm in Gilead, Inc.	Originator of the Harlem Week of Prayer for the Healing of AIDS	804-644-2256	info@balmingilead.org	www.balmingilead.org
Broadway Cares/ Equity Fights AIDS	Awards grants to AIDS service organizations nationwide	212-840-0770	info@bcefa.org	www.bcefa.org
Cable Positive	Uses the resources of the communications industry to raise AIDS awareness and fund AIDS education, research and care.	212-459-1502	info@cablepositive.org	www.cablepositive.org
CDC National Prevention Information Network	Provides technical assistance and publication distribution for organizations and professionals working in HIV/AIDS, STD and TB prevention	1-800-458-5231 AIDS Hotline: 1-800-232-4636	info@cdcnpin.org	www.cdcnpin.org
Centers for AIDS Prevention Studies	Information resource	415-597-9100	CAPS.Web@ucsf.edu	www.caps.ucsf.edu

ORGANIZATION	SERVICES PROVIDED	TELEPHONE	E-MAIL	WEBSITE
Children's AIDS Fund	Dedicated to helping limit the suffering of HIV impacted children through direct assistance and resources	1-888-829-1560	N/A	www.childrensaidsfund.org
Children with AIDS Project of America	Facilitates adoption of HIV-positive children	480-774-9718	jimjenkins@aidskids.org	www.aidskids.org
Commission on Mental and Physical Disability Law	Conducts research and provides training on legal issues regarding disability issues	202-662-1570	N/A	www.abanet.org
Congress of National Black Churches, Inc.	Concerned with HIV/AIDS prevention and care in the African American community in the United States and abroad.	404-571-6300	inquiries@cpjustice.org	www.cpjustice.org
Council of Chief State School Officers Resource Center on Educational Equity HIV Education Project	Assists chief state school officers and state education agencies in providing effective education about HIV/AIDS within comprehensive school health programs	202-408-5505	N/A	www.ccsso.org
Council of Religious AIDS Networks	Dedicated to the promotion of various AIDS issues	202-842-0010	info@aidsfaith.com	www.aidsfaith.com
Dignity/USA	Promotes spiritual development, educational outreach and social reform to gay, lesbian, bisexual and transgender Catholics and their families and friends	202-861-0017	info@dignityusa.org	www.dignityusa.org

ORGANIZATION	SERVICES PROVIDED	TELEPHONE	E-MAIL	WEBSITE
Disability Rights Education and Defense Fund	A national law and policy center dedicated to furthering the civil rights of people with disabilities, such as HIV/AIDS	510-644-2555	info@dredf.org	www.dredf.org
Elton John AIDS Foundation	Provides funding for educational programs and services to people living with HIV/AIDS	310-535-1775	N/A	www.ejaf.org
Gay and Lesbian Medical Association	Combats homophobia in the medical profession and in society and offers support services for HIV-positive healthcare workers	415-255-4547	info@glma.org	www.glma.org
Gay Men's Health Crisis	Gay activist organization	212-367-1000	webmaster@gmhc.org	www.gmhc.org
HIV/AIDS Treatment Information Service	Provides multilingual health information specialists to answer questions on HIV treatment options	1-800-HIV-0440	contactus@aidsinfo.nih.gov	www.hivatis.org
HIV Positive	Provides information and resources to people who are HIV-positive	N/A	N/A	www.hivpositive.com
HIV/AIDS Treatment Information Service	Provides multilingual health information specialists to answer questions on HIV treatment options	1-800-HIV-0440	contactus@aidsinfo.nih.gov	www.hivatis.org

ORGANIZATION	SERVICES PROVIDED	TELEPHONE	E-MAIL	WEBSITE
Human Rights Campaign	Lobbies the federal government on lesbian and gay health issues and promotes sound HIV/AIDS federal policies	800-777-4723	hrc@hrc.org	www.hrc.org
Planned Parenthood Federation of America	Provides testing and treatment for HIV/AIDS and other sexually transmitted infections	1-800-230-PLAN	N/A	www.plannedparenthood.org
Infectious Diseases in Corrections Report	A forum for correctional administrators and HIV/AIDS care provider	401-453-2068	idcrme@gmail.com	www.idcronline.org
Intercultural Family Services, Inc.	Provides culturally competent HIV/AIDS services	215-386-1298	ifsi@ifsinc.org	www.ifsinc.org
International Gay and Lesbian Human Rights Commission	Protects and advances the human rights of all people and communities subject to discrimination	415-255-8680	iglhrc@iglhrc.org	www.iglhrc.org
Join Together Online	Internet resource for communities working to reduce substance abuse	617-437-1500	info@jointogether.org	www.jointogether.org
Metro Teen AIDS	Offers HIV education and prevention services for adolescents and young adults	202-543-9355	atenner@metroteenaids.org	www.newmetroteen.org
Mother's Voices	Promotes public policies that advance AIDS education, prevention, research and treatment	305-347-5467	voicessf@bellsouth.net	www.mothersvoices.org

ORGANIZATION	SERVICES PROVIDED	TELEPHONE	E-MAIL	WEBSITE
NAMES Project Foundation	Custodian of the AIDS Memorial Quilt	415-882-5500	info@aidsquilt.org	www.aidsquilt.org
National AIDS Fund	Provides care and prevention through advocacy, grantmaking, research and education	202-408-4848	kferree@aidsfund.org	www.aidsfund.org
National AIDS Memorial Grove	A living tribute in San Francisco's Golden Gate Park to those lost to AIDS	415-765-0497	info@aidsmemorial.org	www.aidsmemorial.org
National AIDS Treatment Advocacy Project	Provides current HIV drug development, research and treatment information	1-888-26-NATAP	info@natap.org	www.natap.org
National Alliance for Hispanic Health	Provides training and technical assistance in HIV/AIDS prevention program planning and implementation in Hispanic communities	202-387-5000	alliance@hispanichealth.org	www.hispanichealth.org
National Alliance of State and Territorial AIDS Directors	Administers HIV/AIDS health care, prevention and support programs funded by states and federal government	202-434-8090	nastad@nastad.org	www.nastad.org
National Association of County and City Health Officials	Advocates for progressive HIV policy and adequate resources to sustain and enhance prevention, research and care services	202-783-5550	N/A	www.naccho.org

ORGANIZATION	SERVICES PROVIDED	TELEPHONE	E-MAIL	WEBSITE
National Association of People with AIDS	Arranges for HIV-positive and affected educators to speak at engagements nationwide	240-247-0880	info@napwa.org	www.napwa.org
National Black Leadership Commission on AIDS	Coordinates and organizes the volunteers through community development, policymaking and fundraising	800-992-6531	info@nblca.org	www.nblca.org
National Catholic AIDS Network	Clearinghouse of information, provides education and technical assistance, and sponsors a national conference	707-874-3031	info@ncan.org	www.ncan.org
National Center for Youth Law	Support center working to provide adolescents and children with the proper health care and legal services	415-543-3307	info@youthlaw.org	www.youthlaw.org
National Clinicians' Post-Exposure Prophylaxis Hotline (PEPline)	Provides around-the-clock expert guidance in managing healthcare worker exposures to HIV and immediate post-exposure prophylaxis recommendations	1-888-HIV-4911	N/A	www.ucsf.edu/hivcntr/Hotlines/PEPline.html
National Coalition of Hispanic Health and Human Services	Provides training and assistance on HIV/AIDS prevention in Hispanic communities	202-387-5000	alliance@hispanichealth.org	www.cossmho.org

ORGANIZATION	SERVICES PROVIDED	TELEPHONE	E-MAIL	WEBSITE
National Conference of State Legislatures	Produces a variety of HIV/AIDS-related publications and provides research assistance to legislators and staff on HIV/AIDS topics	202-624-5400	ncslnet-admin@ncsl.org	www.ncsl.org
National Council of La Raza AIDS Center	Provides technical assistance and training to reduce the spread of HIV in the Hispanic community	202-785-1670	comments@nclr.org	www.nclr.org
National Education Association Health Information Network	Provides school employees with information on health issues of concern to students and school personnel	202-822-7570	info@neahin.org	www.neahin.org
National Gay and Lesbian Task Force and Policy Institute	Lobbies for gay and lesbian rights issues and AIDS rights issues	202-393-5177	info@thetaskforce.org	www.ngltf.org
National Hemophilia Foundation	Provides information on hemophilia and HIV/AIDS	1-800-42-HANDI	handi@hemophilia.org	www.hemophilia.org
National HIV/AIDS Telephone Consultation Service (Warmline)	Provides expert clinical advice on HIV/AIDS management for health care providers	1-800-933-3413	N/A	www.ucsf.edu/hivcntr/Hotlines/Warmline.html
National HIV Testing Resources	Locates HIV testing sites in communities	N/A	N/A	www.hivtest.org

ORGANIZATION	SERVICES PROVIDED	TELEPHONE	E-MAIL	WEBSITE
National Latina Health Network	Addresses critical public health concerns affecting Latinas and their families	202-965-9633	info@nlhn.net	www.nlhn.net
National Minority AIDS Council	Provides comprehensive assistance to AIDS workers in communities of color	202-483-6622	pkawata@nmac.org	www.nmac.org
National Native American AIDS Prevention Center	Offers treatment services and prevention education to American Indians, Alaska Natives and Native Hawaiians	720-382-2244	information@nnaapc.org	www.nnaapc.org
National Network for Youth	Strives to increase attention to children's issues and key legislation affecting children	202-783-7949	info@NN4Youth.org	www.NN4Youth.org
National Pediatric and Family HIV Resource Center	Provides consultation, technical assistance, and training for health care providers and explores public policy issues related to the care of HIV-positive children	N/A	bbs@thebody.com	www.thebody.org
National Perinatal HIV Consultation and Referral Service (Perinatal Hotline)	Provides around-the-clock advice on indications and interpretations of standard and rapid HIV testing in pregnancy and antiretroviral use in pregnancy, labor and delivery, and postpartum period. Also links HIV-infected pregnant women with appropriate health care	1-888-448-8765	N/A	www.ucsf.edu/hivcntr/Hotlines/Perinatal.html

ORGANIZATION	SERVICES PROVIDED	TELEPHONE	E-MAIL	WEBSITE
National STD/HIV Prevention Training Center Network	CDC-funded regional centers partnered with health departments and universities to increase knowledge and skills of health care professionals in the area of sexual and reproductive health	515-357-7300	N/A	www.stdptc.uc.edu
National Women's Health Network	Clearinghouse for information on women's health	202-347-1140	nwhn@nwhn.org	www.nwhn.org
New Conservatory Theatre Center	Provides age-appropriate HIV prevention education for children ages 5-19 through touring theatre presentations	415-861-4914	email@nctcsf.org	www.nctcsf.org
Pan American Health Organization (PAHO)	Works to strengthen national and local health systems and improve the health of the peoples of the Americas	202-974-3458	publicinfo@paho.org	www.paho.org
Planned Parenthood Federation of America	Provides testing and treatment for HIV/AIDS and other sexually transmitted infections	1-800-230-PLAN	N/A	www.plannedparenthood.org
Project Inform	Provides treatment information and advocacy for HIV-infected individuals	1-415-558-8669	action@projectinform.org	www.projectinform.org
San Francisco AIDS Foundation	Information resource	415-863-2437	feedback@sfaf.org	www.sfaf.org

ORGANIZATION	SERVICES PROVIDED	TELEPHONE	E-MAIL	WEBSITE
Sexuality Information and Education Council of the U.S. (SIECUS)	Provides training, resources, and technical assistance to organizations and individuals around the world which work on sexuality issues and sexual health	212-819-9770	siecus@siecus.org	www.siecus.org
The Body	Information Resource	N/A	N/A	www.thebody.com
The Global Health Council	Largest membership organization in the U.S. advocating for increased funding and visibility for global health issues	202-833-5900	webmaster@globalhealth.org	www.globalhealth.org
The Learning Partnership	Publishes Straight Talk, a magazine-style health education and risk-reduction program for adolescents	914-769-0055	N/A	N/A
UNAIDS	Heads the international response to HIV and tracks HIV/AIDS statistics	+41.22.791.3666	hrm@unaids.org	www.unaids.org
Universal Fellowship of Metropolitan Community Churches HIV/AIDS Ministry Program	Develops, implements and focuses on issues such as HIV/AIDS education, care, prevention.	310-360-8640	info@MCCchurch.net	www.mcchurch.org
Until There's a Cure Foundation	Raises funds for HIV/AIDS care services	800-88-UNTIL	info@utac.org	www.until.org

ORGANIZATION	SERVICES PROVIDED	TELEPHONE	E-MAIL	WEBSITE
Visual AIDS	Volunteer group of art professionals who create and coordinate AIDS awareness programs and provide direct services to artists living with HIV/AIDS	212-627-9855	info@visualaids.org	www.visualaids.org

Sources: Centers for Disease Control and Prevention (CDC)

APPENDIX 2:
DIRECTORY OF GOVERNMENT AGENCIES CONCERNED WITH HIV/AIDS ISSUES

AGENCY	SERVICES PROVIDED	TELEPHONE	E-MAIL	WEBSITE
AIDS.gov	Provides one-stop access to U.S. Government HIV/AIDS information	N/A	contact@AIDS.gov	www.aids.gov
AIDSinfo	Provides the latest federally approved information on HIV/AIDS clinical research, treatment, and medical practice guidelines	1-800-HIV-0440	contactus@aidsinfo.nih.gov	www.aidsinfo.nih.gov
CDC National Prevention Information Network	Provides technical assistance and publication distribution for organizations and professionals working in HIV/AIDS, STD and TB prevention	1-800-458-5231	info@cdcnpin.org	www.cdcnpin.org
Centers for Disease Control and Prevention	Provides answers to questions regarding HIV/AIDS and information on how to protect oneself	1-800-CDC-INFO	cdcinfo@cdc.gov	www.cdc.gov/hiv

AGENCY	SERVICES PROVIDED	TELEPHONE	E-MAIL	WEBSITE
Health Resources and Services Administration	Administers the Ryan White CARE Act, which provides primary health care and support services for people living with HIV/AIDS and supports the education and training of HIV/AIDS health professionals	301-443-6652	N/A	www.hrsa.gov/hab
Medline Plus Health Information	A service of the National Library of Medicine & National Institutes of Health	N/A	N/A	Medlineplus.nim.nih.gov
Substance Abuse and Mental Health Services Administration	Provides information and referrals for HIV/AIDS	1-800-789-2647	N/A	www.samhsa.gov
U.S. Agency for International Development	Administers the U.S.. foreign development assistance program and has committed more than $1.1 billion to HIV/AIDS prevention activities since 1986 in over 50 developing countries worldwide	202-712-1279	N/A	www.eeoc.giv

AGENCY	SERVICES PROVIDED	TELEPHONE	E-MAIL	WEBSITE
United States Conference of Mayors	Provides grants for HIV prevention activities to mayors, community-based organizations and local health departments	202-293-7730	info@usmayors.org	www.usmayors.org/uscm
U.S. Department of Health and Human Services Office for Civil Rights	Works to end discrimination against qualified individuals with handicaps, including AIDS.	202-619-0403	N/A	www.hhs.gov
U.S. Equal Employment Opportunity Commission	Enforces federal antidiscrimination laws such as Title 1 of the Americans with Disabilities Act through investigation, conciliation, litigation, education and technical assistance	202-663-4900	N/A	www.eeoc.giv
White House Office of National AIDS Policy	Provides broad policy guidance and leadership on the Federal government's response to the AIDS epidemic	202-456-2437	N/A	www.whitehouse.gov/ONAP

Source: Centers for Disease Control and Prevention (CDC)

APPENDIX 3:
DIRECTORY OF STATE AIDS HOTLINES

STATE	AIDS HOTLINE
Alabama	In Alabama: 1-800-228-0469 National: 334-206-5364
Alaska	In Alaska: 1-800-478-2437 National: 907-276-4880
Arizona	In Arizona: 1-800-334-1540 National: 602-230-5819
Arkansas	National: 501-661-2408
California	In California: 1-800-367-AIDS In San Francisco and outside California: 415-863-2437 TTY/TTD: 1-888-367-AIDS
Colorado	In Colorado: 1-800-252-2437 Denver Only: 303-782-5186
Connecticut	In Connecticut: 1-800-233-2503 National: 860-509-7800
Delaware	In Delaware: 1-800-422-0429 National: 302-652-6776
Florida	In Florida: 1-800-352-AIDS National: 850-681-9131 Haitian/Creole: 1-800-243-7101 Spanish: 1-800-545-SIDA
Georgia	In Georgia: 1-800-551-2728 National: 404-876-9944
Hawaii	In Hawaii: 1-800-321-1555 National: 1-808-922-1313

STATE	AIDS HOTLINE
Idaho	In Idaho: 1-800-926-2588 National: 208-321-2777
Illinois	In Illinois: 1-800-243-2437 National: 217-785-7165 TTY/TDD: 1-800-782-0423
Indiana	National: 1-800-2332-4636
Iowa	National: 1-800-232-4636
Kansas	National: 785-296-6036
Kentucky	In Kentucky: 502-564-6539
Louisiana	In Louisiana: 1-800-992-4379 National: 504-821-6050 TTY/TDD: 1-877-566-9448
Maine	In Maine: 1-800-851-2437 National: 1-800-775-1267
Maryland	In Maryland: 1-800-638-6252 National: 410-767-5013 Metro DC & VA: 1-800-322-7432 TTY/TDD (Baltimore Only): 410-333-2437 Hispanic AIDS Hotline: 301-949-0945
Massachusetts	In Massachusetts: 1-800-235-2331 National: 617-536-7733 TTY/TDD: 617-437-1672 Youth Only: 1-800-788-1234
Michigan	In Michigan: 1-800-872-2437 National: 313-446-9800 TTY/TDD: 1-800-332-0849 Spanish: 1-800-826-SIDA Teen Line: 1-800-750-8336 Health Care Workers: 1-800-522-0399
Minnesota	In Minnesota: 1-800-248-2437 National: 612-373-2437 TTY/TDD: 1-888-820-2437
Mississippi	In Mississippi: 1-800-826-2961 National: 601-576-7723
Missouri	National: 1-800-533-2437
Montana	Eastern Montana: 1-800-675-2437 Western Montana: 1-800-663-9002
Nebraska	National: 1-800-782-2437

STATE	AIDS HOTLINE
Nevada	In Nevada: 1-800-842-2437 National: 775-684-5900
New Hampshire	In New Hampshire: 1-800-752-2437 National: 603-271-4502
New Jersey	In New Jersey: 1-800-624-2377 National: 973-926-7443
New Mexico	In New Mexico: 1-800-545-2437 National: 505-476-3612
New York	Counseling Hotline: 1-800-872-2777 National: 716-845-3170 Information Hotline: 1-800-541-2437 Spanish Hotline: 1-800-233-SIDA TTY/TDD: 1-800-396-2437 NYC Dept. of Health AIDS Helpline: 1-800-TALK-HIV AIDS Institute Experimental Treatment Info Line: 1-800-633-7444 GMHC Aids Hotline: 212-807-6655 GMHC TDD: 212-645-7470 Body Positive Helpline: 1-800-566-6599 Long Island AIDS Hotline: 516-385-AIDS AIDS Council of Northeastern NY Hotline: 518-445-2437/1-800-201-AIDS
North Carolina	In North Carolina: 1-800-342-2437 National: 919-733-3039
North Dakota	In North Dakota: 1-800-472-2180 National: 701-328-2378
Ohio	In Ohio: 1-800-332-2437 National: 614-466-6374 TTY/TDD: 1-800-332-3889
Oklahoma	In Oklahoma: 1-800-535-2437 National: 918-834-4194
Oregon	In Oregon (area codes 503/206/208): 1-800-777-2437 National: 503-223-2437 Voice/TTY: 503-223-2437
Pennsylvania	In Pennsylvania: 1-800-662-6080 National: 717-783-0573 Critical Path Project Hotline: 215-545-2212 Publication Orders: 215-463-7160
Puerto Rico	In Puerto Rico: 1-800-981-5721 National: 809-765-1010

STATE	AIDS HOTLINE
Rhode Island	National: 1-800-726-3010
South Carolina	In South Carolina: 1-800-322-2437 National: 803-898-0749
South Dakota	In South Dakota: 1-800-592-1861 National: 605-773-3737
Tennessee	In Tennessee: 1-800-525-AIDS National: 615-741-7500
Texas	In Texas: 1-800-299-2437 National: 572-490-2505
Utah	In Utah: 1-800-366-2437 National: 801-487-2100
Vermont	In Vermont: 1-800-882-2437 National: 802-863-7245
Virgin Islands	National: 809-773-2437
Virginia	In Virginia: 1-800-533-4148 National: 804-371-7455 Hispanic Hotline: 1-800-322-7432
Washington	In Washington: 1-800-272-2437 National: 360-236-3466
West Virginia	In West Virginia: 1-800-642-8244 National: 304-558-2950
Wisconsin	In Wisconsin: 1-800-334-2437 National: 414-273-2437
Wyoming	National: 1-800-327-3577

Source: San Francisco AIDS Foundation

APPENDIX 4:
AIDS QUILT PANEL MAKER INFORMATION FORM

PRIMARY PANEL MAKER(S) INFORMATION Please print	OFFICE USE ONLY
Name	Prod. Code
Street	12 X 12 No.
City State ZIP	Date Rec'd.
Phone (eve): (day):	
NAME(S) ON PANEL Please print	The person I made the panel for was my:
FULL NAME(S) IF DIFFERENT FROM ABOVE (Optional)	(relationship)
	Letter ☐ Photo ☐ $
IMPORTANT CITIES This does not mean your panel will automatically be displayed in the cities listed.	Dates on Panel
	I acknowledge that The NAMES Project Foundation is the owner of this panel and any accompanying documents I submit, and I assign to The NAMES Project Foundation any right, title, and interest I may have in such submissions.
My status as a panelmaker is confidential but I understand I will receive The NAMES Project newsletter and other communications from the Foundation.	
☐ I am already on the mailing list ☐ Please do not exchange my name	Signed
Also, I am willing to be contacted by The NAMES Project when:	Dated
☐ Media people are interested in my story or the panel	
☐ Someone requests information about the panel	

PRIMARY PANEL MAKER(S) INFORMATION | Please print

Name

Street

City   State   ZIP

Phone (eve):   (day):

NAME(S) ON PANEL   Please print

FULL NAME(S) IF DIFFERENT FROM ABOVE (Optional)

IMPORTANT CITIES   This does not mean your panel will automatically be displayed in the cities listed.

My status as a panelmaker is confidential but I understand I will receive The NAMES Project newsletter and other communications from the Foundation.

☐ I am already on the mailing list   ☐ Please do not exchange my name

Also, I am willing to be contacted by The NAMES Project when:

☐ Media people are interested in my story or the panel
☐ Someone requests information about the panel

OFFICE USE ONLY

Prod. Code

12 X 12 No.

Date Rec'd.

The person I made the panel for was my:

(relationship)

Letter ☐   Photo ☐ $

Dates on Panel

I acknowledge that The NAMES Project Foundation is the owner of this panel and any accompanying documents I submit, and I assign to The NAMES Project Foundation any right, title, and interest I may have in such submissions.

Signed

Dated

AIDS Law

APPENDIX 5:
DIRECTORY OF NAMES PROJECT FOUNDATION CHAPTERS

REGION/ CHAPTER	ADDRESS	TELEPHONE/FAX	E-MAIL	WEBSITE
Region 1 Rep: Eric Miller	Areas Covered: AL, AR, DE, FL, GA, KY, LA, MD, MS, NC, SC, TN, TX, VA, WV	N/A	delocartier@aol.com	N/A
Region 1 Delaware	Delaware HIV Consortium 100 West 10th Street Suite 415 Wilmington, DE 19801	Tel: 302-654-5471 Fax: N/A	mpollock@delawarehiv.org	N/A
Region 1 Northeast Florida	2024 Gilmore Street Jacksonville, FL 32204	Tel: N/A Fax: 904-394-4545	j.miller@firstcoatpride.com	N/A
Region 1 South Florida	P.O. Box 11294 Fort Lauderdale, FL 33339	Tel: 702-265-3876 Fax: N/A	panels123@aol.com	www.namesprojects outhflorida.org
Region 1 Georgia	637 Hoke Street NW Atlanta, GA 30318-4315	Tel: 404-688-5500 Fax: 404-688-5552	displays@aidsquilt.org	www.aidsquilt.org
Region 1 Texas	P.O. Box 306 Frisco, TX 75034	Tel: 972-200-9411 Fax: N/A	namesproject@ntaac.org	www.namesproject. ntaac.org

REGION/ CHAPTER	ADDRESS	TELEPHONE/FAX	E-MAIL	WEBSITE
Region 1 West Virginia	P.O. Box 6360 Wheeling, WV 26003	Tel: 304-232-6822 Fax: 740-695-3252	jayadams3@sbcglobal.net	N/A
Region 2 Rep: Jim Schiefelbein	Areas Covered: CT, MA, ME, MI, IL, IN, NH, NJ, NY, OH, PA, RI, VT, WI	N/A	Jim.Schiefelbein@ bairdwarner.com	N/A
Region 2 Illinois	2855 N. Lincoln Avenue Chicago, IL 60657	Tel: 773-472-6469 Fax: 773-472-3945	names@centeronhalsted. org	www.namesproject chicago.org
Region 2 Indiana	1350 N. Pennsylvania Street Indianapolis, IN 46202	Tel: 317-632-0123 Fax: 317-632-4362	edalexander@damien.org	N/A
Region 2 Massachusetts (Boston)	N/A	Tel: 404-688-5550 Fax: N/A	N/A	www.aidsquilt.org
Region 2 Maine	P.O. Box 2169 Ogunquit, ME 03907	Tel: 207-646-1195 Fax: N/A	kbartuka@gwi.net	N/A
Region 2 Michigan	22331 Woodward Avenue Ferndale, MI 48220	Tel: 248-691-1122 Fax: N/A	contactus@namesproject- michigan.org	www.namesproject- michigan.org
Region 2 Central New Jersey	P.O. Box 716 New Brunswick, NJ 08903	Tel: 732-249-3933 Fax: N/A	namespcnj@aol.com	N/A

REGION/ CHAPTER	ADDRESS	TELEPHONE/FAX	E-MAIL	WEBSITE
Region 2 Northern New Jersey	P.O. Box 85 Paramus, NJ 06753	Tel: 201-265-0600 Fax: N/A	info@NAMESNNJ.org	www.NAMESNNJ.org
Region 2 New York (NYC)	N/A	Tel: 212-234-0334 Fax: N/A	N/A	N/A
Region 2 New York	225 Lark Street Albany, NY 12210	Tel: 518-465-0595 Fax: N/A	AIDSQuiltNY@aol.com	www.AIDSQuiltNY.org
Region 3 Rep: Raymond Chance	Areas Covered: AZ, CA, CO, IA, ID, KS, MN, MO, MT, ND, NE, NM, NV, OK, OR, SD, UT, WA, WY		raychance@cox.net	N/A
Region 3 California (Los Angeles)	N/A	Tel: 323-655-5809 Fax: N/A	rolandolirra@spcglobal.net	N/A
Region 3 Hawaii	1710 #1004 Makiki Street Honolulu, HI 96822	Tel: 808-943-7961 Fax: N/A	gachong2@aol.com	N/A
Region 3 Missouri	P.O. Box 15102 St. Louis, MO 63110	Tel: 314-353-7772 Fax: N/A	purrfect@hotmail.com	N/A
Region 3 Oklahoma	205 W. King Street Tulsa, OK 74106	Tel: 918-663-0820 Fax: N/A	N/A	www.tulsaquilt.org

Source: NAMES Project Foundation

APPENDIX 6:
DIRECTORY OF NAMES PROJECT INTERNATIONAL AFFILIATES

COUNTRY	ADDRESS	TELEPHONE/FAX	E-MAIL	WEBSITE
Argentina	Proyecto de los Nombres Argentina Proyecto de Asociacion de Lucha contra el Sida Santiago del Estero 454 9 "35" Buenos Aires 1075 Argentina	Tel: (54) 1-383-2212 Fax: (54) 1-384-6474	soldar@cvtci.com.ar	N/A
Austria	Names Project Wien c/o HOSI Wien A-1020 Vienna, Austria	Tel: +43-1-216 66 04 Fax: +43-1-216 66 04	office@namesproject.at	www.namesproject.at
Australia	The Quilt Project Sydney P.O. Box 862 Darlinghurst NSW 2010 Australia	Tel: (61) 2-360-7669 Fax: (61) 2-331-7628	douglas@rainbow.net.au	N/A
Belgium	Namesproject Belgium P/A Sensoa - "Geef om aids-fonds" Vlaanderen Kipdorpvest 48 A 2000 Antwerp, Belgium	Tel: (32) 3/238.68.68 Fax: (32) 3/248.42.90	Patrick.reyntiens@sensoa.be	N/A

COUNTRY	ADDRESS	TELEPHONE/FAX	E-MAIL	WEBSITE
Brazil	Associacao IVAN Rua Joaquim Antunes #570-101, Pinheiros Sao Paulo, SP, Brazil	Tel: (55) 11-280-3552 Fax: (55) 11-280-3552	N/A	N/A
Canada	NAMES Project - Canada 3544 Acadia Street Halifax B3K 3P2, Canada	Tel: 902-454-5158 Fax: 902-424-4727	larrybaxter@ns.sympatico.ca	W2ww.quilt.ca
Chile	Arpillera Corporacion Chilena de Prevencion del SIDA Casilla 49, Correo 22 Santiago, Chile	Tel: (56) 2-222-8356 Fax: N/A	chiliads@cchps.tie.cl	www.sidaccion.cl
Cuba	Proyecto MEMORIAS C/o Grupo de Prevencion de SIDA La Hubana, Cuba	Tel: (53) 7-412-177 Fax: N/A	qpsida@iinformed.sid.cu	N/A
Denmark	Navneprojektet I Danmark c/o Kafe Knud Skindergade 26 1159 Kobenhavn K, Denmark	Tel: (45) 3391-1114 Fax: N/A	N/A	N/A
France	Patchwork des Noms c/o Le Tipi 26, Rue de la Bibiotheque 13001 Marseille, France	Tel: (33) 4-91811250 Fax: (33) 4-91788483	patchw13@aol.com	N/A
Germany	Deutscher AIDS-Quilt c/o Munchner AIDS-Hilfe e.v. Lindwurmstrasse 71 80337 Munchen, Germany	Tel: (49) 89-157-3752 Fax: (49) 89-5446-4711	qwilliam@nw80.cip.fak14. uni-muenchen.de	N/A

COUNTRY	ADDRESS	TELEPHONE/FAX	E-MAIL	WEBSITE
Guam	Memorial Quilt Taotao Guam c/o Coral Life Foundation P.O. Box 5183 Agana, Guam 96910 USA	Tel: (671) 646-2876 Fax: (671) 734-1475	bprovido@ns.gov.gu	N/A
Guatemala	Proyecto Nombres-Guatemala c/o APAES Solidaridad Apartado Postal 1636 Guatemala City, Guatemala	Tel: (502) 232-7649 Fax: (502) 232-7649	apaes@starnet.net.gt	N/A
Hong Kong	The Hong Kong AIDS Memorial Quilt Project GPO Box 7373 Hong Kong SAR, China	Tel: (852) 2870 1222 Fax: (852) 2870 3623	sexed@teenaids.org.hk	TeenAids.org.hk
Ireland	The Irish Names Quilt 53 Parnell Sq. West Dublin 1, Ireland	Tel: (353) 1-679-2401 Fax: (353) 1-677-9939	N/A	N/A
Israel	Proyect HaShemot/The NAMES Project Israel P.O. Box 16427 61163 Tel Aviv, Israel	Tel: (972) 3-672-0022 Fax: (972) 3-672-0022	quilt@netvision.net.il	www.geocities.com/ heartland/prairie/1214
Italy	Names Project Italy c/o Associazione Solidarieta AIDS-ASA Via Arena, 25 Milano 20123, Italy	Tel: (39) 2-5810-7084 Fax: (39) 2-5810-6490	asamilan@mbox.vol.it	N/A

COUNTRY	ADDRESS	TELEPHONE/FAX	E-MAIL	WEBSITE
Japan	Memorial Quilt Japan Plaza Shin-Osaka 216 1-6-60 Nishimiyahara, Yodogawa-ku, Osaka 532 Japan	Tel: (81) 6-350-9286 Fax: (81) 6-350-9287	N/A	N/A
Mexico	La Manta de Mexico Guanajuato 131 Colonia Roma C.P. 067000, Mexico, D.F.	Tel: (55) 85-96-35-35 Fax: (55) 55-74-13-73	lamanta@lamanta.org	www.lamanta.org
Netherlands	Dutch NAMES Project P.O. Box 15847 1001 NH Amsterdam Amsterdam NH, Netherlands	Tel: (31) 20 616 0160 Fax: (31) 20 616 1200	hivhvn@xs4all.nl	N/A
New Zealand	The AIDS Quilt Aotearoa P.O. Box 7024 Wellesley Street Auckland, New Zealand	Tel: (64) 9-309-5560 Fax: (64) 9-302-2338	N/A	N/A
Nigeria	Nigeria AIDS Memorial Quilt Project 127 Ndidem Ussang Iso Calabar, Cross River State Nigeria	Tel: (234) 87-224836 Fax: (234) 87-220-143	N/A	N/A
Northern Ireland	The NAMES Project Northern Ireland C/o The Centre at the Warehouse 7 James Street Belfast, BT2-8DN Northern Ireland	Tel: (44) 1232-249-268 Fax: (44) 1232-329-845	N/A	N/A

COUNTRY	ADDRESS	TELEPHONE/FAX	E-MAIL	WEBSITE
Peru	Arpillera de Nombres de Peru Via Libre Asociacion de Lucha contra el SIDA Jr. Paraguay 478 Lima 1, Peru	Tel: (51) 1-433-1396 Fax: (51) 1-433-1579	sida@vialibre.org.pe	N/A
Philippines	NAMES Project Quilt Philippines 1066 Remedios Corner Singalong Malate 1004 Manila, Philippines	Tel: 632-524-0924 Fax: 632-522-3431	nenetgem@pacific.net.ph	N/A
Poland	Polish NAMES Project c/o UNDP Warsaw P.O. Box1 Warsaw 12, Poland	Tel: N/A Fax: N/A	joanna.kazana@undp.org	N/A
Portugal	Movimento IbUrico Quilt PortuguUs c/o Associacao ILGA-Portugal Rua de Sao Lazaaro, 88 1150 Lisboa, Portugal	Tel: N/A Fax: N/A	joanna.kazana@undp.org	N/A
Romania	NAMES Project Romania c/o Asociata Romana Anti-SIDA Bulevardul Garii Obor, 23, Et. 2, ap 8, Sector 2 72314 Bucuresti, Romania	Tel: (40) 1-252-4141 Fax: (40) 1-252-4141	aras@home.ro	N/A

COUNTRY	ADDRESS	TELEPHONE/FAX	E-MAIL	WEBSITE
Russia	The Russian NAMES Fund 129110, 52/55 Bolshaya Pereyaslavskaya Street stroenie 1, office 21 Moscow, Russia	Tel: (7) 095-933-4233 Fax: (7) 095-933-4233	N/A	www.aids.ru
South Africa	The NAMES Project Cape Town c/o ATICC P.O. Box 2815 Cape Town 8000, South Africa	Tel: (27) 21-400-3327 Fax: (27) 21-419-5248	cajacobs@ctcc.org.za	N/A
Spain	Projecte dels NOMS-Sida Escudellers Blancs, 1, Baixos 08002 Barcelona, Spain	Tel: 34 93 318 20 56 Fax: 34 93 317 82 06	pdn@hispanosida.com	N/A
Suriname	Stichting MAMIO Namen Projekt P.O. Box 8183 Paramaribo, Suriname	Tel: (597) 474-607 Fax: (597) 474-607	reichart@sr.net	N/A
Sweden	The NAMES Project Sweden c/o Noahs Ark-Red Cross Foundation Drottninggatan 61 111 21 Stockholm, Sweden	Tel: (46) 8-700-4623 Fax: (46) 8-700-4610	info@noahsark.redcross.se	N/A
Switzerland	NAMES Project Switzerland NIEUWE ADRES ZIE MAILTJE AAN KOKKIE	Tel: (41) 1-273-4242 Fax: N/A	N/A	N/A

COUNTRY	ADDRESS	TELEPHONE/FAX	E-MAIL	WEBSITE
Taiwan, ROC	Taiwan AIDS Memorial Quilt Project c/o Chinese Society of Preventive Medicine Living with Hope Organization P.O. Box 2-43 Pei Tow, Taipei, Taiwan	Tel: (886) 2-827-0576 Fax: (886) 2-827-0576	arthur@ym.edu.tx	N/A
Thailand	Concrete House 57/60 Tivanod Road Nonta Theburi, 11000 Thailand	Tel: (662) 526-8311 Fax: (662) 526-3294	empower@mozart.inet.co.th	N/A
Trinidad & Tobago	Artists Against AIDS p/a ambassade van Nederland P.O. Box 870 Port-of-Spain	Tel: (868) 625-0632 Fax: (868) 625-0632	N/A	N/A
Uganda	The AIDS Support Organisation (TASO) P.O. Box 10443 Kampala, Uganda	Tel: (256) 41-567-637 Fax: (256) 41-530-412	taso@mukla.gn.apc.org	N/A
United Kingdom	NAMES Project (UK) c/o Crusaid 1-5 Curtain Road London EC2A 3JX United Kingdom	Tel: (44) 207 539 3880 Fax: (44) 207 539 3890	projects@crusaid.org.uk	www.crusaid.org.uk

COUNTRY	ADDRESS	TELEPHONE/FAX	E-MAIL	WEBSITE
Venezuela	Fundacion MAROZO CCS 1144/ P.O. Box 02-5323 Miami, Florida, 33102-5323 USA	Tel: (58) 2-238-6144 Fax: (58) 2-239-7896	barmarer@ccs.internet.ve	N/A
Zambia	Zambia AIDS Memorial Quilt c/o UNZA/IAS Bo 30900 Lusaka, Zambia	Tel: (260) 1-294-131 Fax: (260) 1-237-070	imwanza@zamnet.zm	N/A

Source: NAMES Project Foundation

APPENDIX 7:
WEB ADDRESSES FOR STATE HIV/AIDS SURVEILLANCE REPORTS

STATE	AIDS HOTLINE
Alabama	http://www.adph.org/AIDS/default.asp?TemplateNbr=3&DeptID= 96&TemplateId=3575
Alaska	http://www.epi.hss.state.ak.us/bulletins/docs/b2006_09.pdf
Arizona	http://www.azdhs.gov/phs/hiv/hiv_epi.htm
Arkansas	http://www.healthyarkansas.com/stats/hiv_aids/063006_report.pdf
California	http://www.dhs.ca.gov/AIDS/Statistics/default.htm
Colorado	http://www.cdphe.state.co.us/dc/HIVandSTD/index.html
Connecticut	http://www.dph.state.ct.us/BCH/infectiousdise/2003/finalpages/aids_surv_home_Z.htm
Delaware	http://www.dhss.delaware.gov/dhss/dph/epi/disstatshiv.html
Florida	http://www.doh.state.fl.us/Disease_ctrl/aids/trends/trends.html
Georgia	http://health.state.ga.us/programs/stdhiv/index.asp
Hawaii	http://www.state.hi.us/health/healthy-lifestyles/std-aids/aboutus/prg-aids/aids_rep/index.htm
Idaho	http://www.healthandwelfare.idaho.gov/site/3563/default.aspx
Illinois	http://www.idph.state.il.us/aids/stats.htm
Indiana	http://www.in.gov/isdh/programs/hivstd/quarterly/quarterly.htm

STATE	AIDS HOTLINE
Iowa	http://www.idph.state.ia.us/adper/hiv_aids_programs.asp#surveillance
Kansas	http://www.kdheks.gov/hiv/index.html
Kentucky	http://chfs.ky.gov/dph/epi/stats.htm
Louisiana	http://www.dhh.louisiana.gov/offices/?ID=264
Maine	http://www.maine.gov/dhhs/boh/ddc/data_statistics_surveillance.htm
Maryland	http://www.dhmh.state.md.us/AIDS/Data&Statistics/statistics.htm
Massachusetts	http://www.state.ma.us/dph/cdc/aids/aidsprog.htm
Michigan	http://www.michigan.gov/mdch/0,1607,7-132-2944_5320_5331---,00.html
Minnesota	http://www.health.state.mn.us/divs/idepc/diseases/hiv/hivstatistics.html
Mississippi	http://www.msdh.state.ms.us/msdhsite/indexcfm/14,0,150,htm
Missouri	http://www.dhss.mo.gov/HIV_STD_AIDS/Data.html
Montana	http://www.dphhs.mt.gov/PHSD/Communicable-disease/commun-disease-index.shtml
Nebraska	http://www.hhs.state.ne.us/dpc/HIV.htm
Nevada	http://health2k.state.nv.us/hiv/survey/special.htm
New Hampshire	http://www.dhhs.nh.gov/DHHS/CDCS/LIBRARY/Data-Statistical+Report/hiv-aids-report.htm
New Jersey	http://www.state.nj.us/health/aids/aidsqtr.htm
New Mexico	http://www.health.state.nm.us/hiv-aids.html
New York	http://www.health.state.ny.us/diseases/aids/statistics/index.htm
North Carolina	http://www.epi.state.nc.us/epi/hiv/surveillance.html
North Dakota	http://www.ndhiv.com/resources/
Ohio	http://www.odh.ohio.gov/healthStats/disease/hivcov.aspx
Oklahoma	http://www.health.state.ok.us/program/hivstd/epi/stats.htm
Oregon	http://oregon.gov/DHS/ph/hst/index.shtml
Pennsylvania	http://www.health.state.pa.us/hiv-epi/extranet1.1/index.htm

STATE	AIDS HOTLINE
Rhode Island	http://www.health.ri.gov/hiv/data.php
South Carolina	http://www.dhec.sc.gov/health/disease/stdhiv/ surveillance.htm
South Dakota	http://www.state.sd.us/doh/Disease/stats.htm
Tennessee	http://www.coetenn.com/IndexTNHIVdata.htm
Texas	http://www.dshs.state.tx.us/hivstd/default.shtm
Utah	http://health.utah.gov/cdc/sp.htm
Vermont	http://healthvermont.gov/prevent/aids/quarter/reports.aspx
Virginia	http://www.vdh.state.va.us/std/datahome2.asp
Washington	http://www.doh.wa.gov/cfh/HIV_AIDS/Prev_Edu/Statistics.htm
West Virginia	http://www.wvdhhr.org/idep/aids.asp
Wisconsin	http://www.dhfs.state.wi.us/aids-hiv/Stats/index.htm
Wyoming	http://wdhfs.state.wy.us/hiv

Source: Centers for Disease Control and Prevention

APPENDIX 8:
ESTIMATED NUMBER OF AIDS CASES, BY AGE AT DIAGNOSIS AND YEAR OF DIAGNOSIS FROM 50 STATES AND DISTRICT OF COLUMBIA (2001–2005)

AGE AT DIAGNOSIS	2001	2002	2003	2004	2005
Under 13	121	105	71	50	68
13–14	82	67	78	83	86
15–19	266	318	309	341	447
20–24	1,305	1,404	1,595	1,703	1,836
25–29	3,143	3,149	3,121	3,327	3,407
30–34	6,101	5,737	5,663	5,355	5,122
35–39	8,419	8,288	8,294	7,448	7,246
40–44	7,287	7,472	7,839	8,080	8,210
45–49	5,257	5,406	5,804	5,763	6,418
50–54	3,096	3,293	3,470	3,674	3,935
55–59	1,492	1,603	1,737	1,914	2,064
60–64	790	877	889	939	967
65 and Over	720	689	795	845	801

Source: Centers for Disease Control and Prevention

APPENDIX 9:
ESTIMATED NUMBER OF AIDS CASES, BY RACE/ETHNICITY AND YEAR OF DIAGNOSIS FROM 50 STATES AND THE DISTRICT OF COLUMBIA (2001–2005)

RACE/ETHNICITY	2001	2002	2003	2004	2005
White, Not Hispanic	11,001	11,274	11,254	11,520	11,780
Black, Not Hispanic	19,465	19,559	20,224	19,963	20,187
Hispanic	6,847	6,711	7,291	7,099	7,676
Asian/Pacific Islander	374	427	461	471	483
American Indian/Alaska Native	166	181	186	188	182

Source: Centers for Disease Control and Prevention

APPENDIX 10: ESTIMATED NUMBER OF AIDS CASES, BY TRANSMISSION CATEGORY/MALE ADULT OR ADOLESCENT AND YEAR OF DIAGNOSIS FROM 50 STATES AND THE DISTRICT OF COLUMBIA (2001–2005)

TRANSMISSION CATEGORY	2001	2002	2003	2004	2005
Male-to-Male Sexual Contact	15,294	15,764	16,448	16,660	17,230
Injection Drug Use	5,948	5,682	5,579	5,243	5,441
Male-to-Male Sexual Contact and Injection Drug Use	2,104	1,990	2,002	1,942	2,018
High-Risk Heterosexual Contact	4,293	4,567	4,616	4,707	4,797
Other	269	272	246	265	280
SUBTOTAL	27,908	28,276	28,891	28,817	29,766

Source: Centers for Disease Control and Prevention

APPENDIX 11:
ESTIMATED NUMBER OF AIDS CASES, BY TRANSMISSION CATEGORY/FEMALE ADULT OR ADOLESCENT AND YEAR OF DIAGNOSIS FROM 50 STATES AND THE DISTRICT OF COLUMBIA (2001–2005)

TRANSMISSION CATEGORY	2001	2002	2003	2004	2005
Injection Drug Use	3,099	2,911	2,971	2,961	2,940
High-Risk Heterosexual Contact	6,730	6,895	7,501	7,447	7,591
Other	220	221	232	248	243
SUBTOTAL	10,049	10,027	10,704	10,656	10,774

Source: Centers for Disease Control and Prevention

APPENDIX 12:
ESTIMATED NUMBER OF AIDS CASES, BY REGION OF RESIDENCE AND YEAR OF DIAGNOSIS FROM 50 STATES AND DISTRICT OF COLUMBIA (2001–2005)

REGION	2001	2002	2003	2004	2005
Northeast	11,273	10,292	10,955	10,452	11,529
Midwest	3,929	4,126	4,282	4,225	4,862
South	16,571	17,301	18,014	18,761	18,115
West	6,306	6,689	6,414	6,086	6,102

Source: Centers for Disease Control and Prevention

APPENDIX 13:
TOP 10 STATES/DEPENDENT AREAS WITH THE HIGHEST REPORTED NUMBER OF AIDS CASES (IN 2005)

STATE/DEPENDENT AREA	# OF AIDS CASES IN 2005
NEW YORK	6,299
FLORIDA	4,960
CALIFORNIA	4,088
TEXAS	3,113
GEORGIA	2,333
ILLINOIS	1,922
MARYLAND	1,595
PENNSYLVANIA	1,510
NEW JERSEY	1,278
PUERTO RICO	1,033

Source: National Center for HIV, STD and TB Prevention

APPENDIX 14:
TOP 10 STATES/DEPENDENT AREAS WITH THE HIGHEST REPORTED CUMULATIVE NUMBER OF AIDS CASES (THROUGH 2005)

STATE/DEPENDENT AREA	# OF CUMULATIVE AIDS CASES THROUGH 2005
NEW YORK	172,377
CALIFORNIA	139,019
FLORIDA	100,809
TEXAS	67,227
NEW JERSEY	48,431
ILLINOIS	32,595
PENNSYLVANIA	31,977
GEORGIA	30,405
MARYLAND	29,116
PUERTO RICO	29,092

Source: National Center for HIV, STD and TB Prevention

APPENDIX 15:
ESTIMATED NUMBER OF AIDS DEATHS, BY AGE AT DEATH AND YEAR OF DEATH FROM 50 STATES AND DISTRICT OF COLUMBIA (2001–2005)

AGE AT DEATH	2001	2002	2003	2004	2005
Under 13	47	25	23	15	7
13–14	3	9	7	14	14
15–19	44	38	38	38	42
20–24	206	152	163	188	157
25–29	612	555	531	509	457
30–34	1,672	1,451	1,328	1,208	1,102
35–39	3,145	2,922	2,889	2,604	2,129
40–44	3,714	3,527	3,682	3,655	3,371
45–49	3,035	3,231	3,355	3,479	3,261
50–54	2,082	2,279	2,480	2,634	2,635
55–59	1,098	1,174	1,371	1,508	1,529
60–64	624	602	732	755	805
65 and Over	698	675	805	845	808

Source: Centers for Disease Control and Prevention

APPENDIX 16:
ESTIMATED NUMBER OF AIDS DEATHS, BY RACE/ETHNICITY AND YEAR OF DEATH FROM 50 STATES AND THE DISTRICT OF COLUMBIA (2001–2005)

RACE/ETHNICITY	2001	2002	2003	2004	2005
White, Not Hispanic	5,239	5,153	5,263	5,137	5,006
Black, Not Hispanic	9,085	8,927	9,077	9,302	8,562
Hispanic	2,436	2,306	2,774	2,664	2,444
Asian/Pacific Islander	99	93	88	113	97
American Indian/Alaska Native	79	84	75	85	81

Source: Centers for Disease Control and Prevention

APPENDIX 17:
ESTIMATED NUMBER OF AIDS DEATHS, BY TRANSMISSION CATEGORY/MALE ADULT OR ADOLESCENT AND YEAR OF DEATH FROM 50 STATES AND THE DISTRICT OF COLUMBIA (2001–2005)

TRANSMISSION CATEGORY	2001	2002	2003	2004	2005
Male-to-Male Sexual Contact	5,995	5,867	6,111	6,078	5,929
Injection Drug Use	3,749	3,662	3,759	3,570	3,159
Male-to-Male Sexual Contact and Injection Drug Use	1,342	1,273	1,354	1,314	1,364
High-Risk Heterosexual Contact	1,485	1,434	1,554	1,729	1,584
Other	169	163	156	136	104
SUBTOTAL	12,740	12,400	12,934	12,826	12,140

Source: Centers for Disease Control and Prevention

APPENDIX 18:
ESTIMATED NUMBER OF AIDS DEATHS, BY TRANSMISSION CATEGORY/FEMALE ADULT OR ADOLESCENT AND YEAR OF DEATH FROM 50 STATES AND THE DISTRICT OF COLUMBIA (2001–2005)

TRANSMISSION CATEGORY	2001	2002	2003	2004	2005
Injection Drug Use	1,829	1,876	1,916	1,959	1,651
High-Risk Heterosexual Contact	2,258	2,225	2,400	2,531	2,413
Other	86	84	94	77	64
SUBTOTAL	4,172	4,185	4,411	4,567	4,128

Source: Centers for Disease Control and Prevention

APPENDIX 19:
ESTIMATED NUMBER OF AIDS DEATHS, BY REGION OF RESIDENCE AND YEAR OF DEATH FROM 50 STATES AND DISTRICT OF COLUMBIA (2001–2005)

REGION	2001	2002	2003	2004	2005
Northeast	5,091	5,047	5,376	4,904	3,948
Midwest	1,682	1,675	1,655	1,619	1,541
South	7,469	7,361	7,776	8,353	8,240
West	2,738	2,559	2,597	2,577	2,588

Source: Centers for Disease Control and Prevention

APPENDIX 20:
ESTIMATED NUMBER OF PERSONS LIVING WITH AIDS, BY AGE AND YEAR FROM 50 STATES AND DISTRICT OF COLUMBIA (2001–2005)

AGE AT END OF YEAR	2001	2002	2003	2004	2005
Under 13	2,641	2,303	1,998	1,670	1,393
13–14	620	689	753	802	793
15–19	1,266	1,493	1,722	2,002	2,301
20–24	3,765	3,926	4,334	4,727	5,261
25–29	13,036	12,739	12,805	13,195	13,924
30–34	37,342	35,669	34,017	32,335	30,573
35–39	71,123	70,411	68,521	65,598	63,441
40–44	75,036	80,881	86,788	91,981	95,415
45–49	58,853	65,334	71,992	78,130	85,572
50–54	36,042	41,706	47,343	53,921	60,374
55–59	17,042	20,416	24,484	28,739	34,167
60–64	8,166	9,833	11,451	13,474	15,642
65 and Over	6,651	7,851	9,304	11,009	13,018

Source: Centers for Disease Control and Prevention

APPENDIX 21:
ESTIMATED NUMBER OF PERSONS LIVING WITH AIDS, BY RACE/ETHNICITY AND YEAR FROM 50 STATES AND THE DISTRICT OF COLUMBIA (2001–2005)

RACE/ETHNICITY	2001	2002	2003	2004	2005
White, Not Hispanic	124,389	130,510	136,501	142,884	149,658
Black, Not Hispanic	141,904	152,536	163,683	174,363	185,988
Hispanic	59,466	63,871	68,388	72,823	78,054
Asian/Pacific Islander	2,825	3,158	3,532	3,891	4,276
American Indian/Alaska Native	1,169	1,266	1,378	1,481	1,581

Source: Centers for Disease Control and Prevention

APPENDIX 22:
ESTIMATED NUMBER OF PERSONS LIVING WITH AIDS, BY TRANSMISSION CATEGORY/MALE ADULT OR ADOLESCENT AND YEAR FROM 50 STATES AND THE DISTRICT OF COLUMBIA (2001–2005)

TRANSMISSION CATEGORY	2001	2002	2003	2004	2005
Male-to-Male Sexual Contact	149,245	159,143	169,479	180,061	191,362
Injection Drug Use	56,070	58,089	59,909	61,582	63,864
Male-to-Male Sexual Contact and Injection Drug Use	23,313	24,030	24,678	25,307	25,961
High-Risk Heterosexual Contact	24,398	27,531	30,593	33,571	36,784
Other	3,650	3,760	3,849	3,979	4,154
SUBTOTAL	256,676	272,553	288,509	304,500	322,125

Source: Centers for Disease Control and Prevention

APPENDIX 23:
ESTIMATED NUMBER OF PERSONS LIVING WITH AIDS, BY TRANSMISSION CATEGORY/FEMALE ADULT OR ADOLESCENT AND YEAR FROM 50 STATES AND THE DISTRICT OF COLUMBIA (2001–2005)

TRANSMISSION CATEGORY	2001	2002	2003	2004	2005
Injection Drug Use	27,140	28,176	29,230	30,232	31,521
High-Risk Heterosexual Contact	42,074	46,743	51,844	56,760	61,938
Other	1,875	2,012	2,149	2,321	2,500
SUBTOTAL	71,089	76,930	83,224	89,313	95,959

Source: Centers for Disease Control and Prevention

APPENDIX 24:
ESTIMATED NUMBER OF CHILDREN UNDER 13 LIVING WITH AIDS, BY TRANSMISSION CATEGORY AND YEAR FROM 50 STATES AND THE DISTRICT OF COLUMBIA (2001–2005)

TRANSMISSION CATEGORY	2001	2002	2003	2004	2005
Perinatal	3,580	3,631	3,648	3,640	3,661
Other	134	132	127	126	126
SUBTOTAL	3,714	3,763	3,775	3,766	3,787

Source: Centers for Disease Control and Prevention

APPENDIX 25:
ESTIMATED NUMBER OF PERSONS LIVING WITH AIDS, BY REGION OF RESIDENCE/YEAR FROM 50 STATES AND THE DISTRICT OF COLUMBIA (2001–2005)

REGION	2001	2002	2003	2004	2005
Northeast	102,684	107,929	113,508	119,055	126,637
Midwest	33,992	36,443	39,070	41,675	44,997
South	127,418	137,359	147,597	158,005	167,880
West	67,389	71,519	75,337	78,845	82,360

Source: Centers for Disease Control and Prevention

APPENDIX 26:
ESTIMATED NUMBER OF GLOBAL HIV/AIDS DIAGNOSES AND AIDS DEATHS (2007)

STATUS	ESTIMATE	RANGE
PEOPLE LIVING WITH HIV/AIDS	33.2 million	30.6-36.1 million
ADULTS LIVING WITH HIV/AIDS	30.8 million	28.2-33.6 million
WOMEN LIVING WITH HIV/AIDS	15.4 million	13.9-16.6 million
CHILDREN LIVING WITH HIV/AIDS	2.5 million	2.2-2.6 million
PEOPLE NEWLY INFECTED WITH HIV	2.5 million	1.8-4.1 million
ADULTS NEWLY INFECTED WITH HIV	2.1 million	1.4-3.6 million
CHILDREN NEWLY INFECTED WITH HIV	0.42 million	0.35-0.54 million
AIDS DEATHS	2.1 million	1.9-2.4 million
ADULT AIDS DEATHS	1.7 million	1.6-2.1 million
CHILD AIDS DEATHS	0.33 million	0.31-0.38 million

Source: UNAIDS/WHO Epidemic Update (November 2007)

APPENDIX 27:
INFORMED CONSENT TO PERFORM AN HIV TEST

Informed Consent to Perform an HIV Test

New York State Department of Health
AIDS Institute

The decision to have an HIV test is voluntary. In order to have an HIV test in New York State, you must give your consent in writing on the bottom of this form.

Testing for HIV Infection Testing Methods:

There are a number of tests that can be done to show if you are infected with HIV, the virus that causes AIDS. Your provider or counselor can provide specific information on these tests. These tests involve collecting and testing blood, urine or oral fluid. The most common test for HIV is the HIV antibody test.

Meaning of HIV Test Results:

• A negative result on the HIV antibody test most likely means that you are not infected with HIV, but it may not show recent infection. If you think you have been exposed to HIV, you should take the test again three months after the last possible exposure.

• A positive result on the test means that you are infected with HIV and can infect others.

• Sometimes the HIV antibody test result is not clearly positive or negative, or may be a preliminary result. Your provider or counselor will explain this result, and may ask that you give your consent for further testing.

Confidential or Anonymous HIV Testing:

When you decide to have an HIV antibody test, you may choose either a confidential or an anonymous test.

• If you want your test result to become part of your medical record so it can be used for your medical care, you can have a confidential test done. A confidential test requires that you provide your name.

• If you do not want anyone to know your test results or that you were tested, you can have an anonymous test at an anonymous test site. You will not be asked your name, address or any other identifying information.

• If you receive an HIV positive test result at an anonymous test site approved by the NYS Department of Health, you will have the option of changing your test result to confidential by attaching your name to the test result. This will allow your test result to become part of your medical record.

Benefits to Testing:

There are many benefits to having an HIV test and knowing if you are infected.

If you receive an HIV negative test result:

• Your provider or counselor will tell you how to protect yourself from getting infected with HIV in the future.

If you receive an HIV positive test result:

• Your provider can give you medical care and treatment that can help you stay healthy and can manage your HIV illness.

• Your provider or counselor can tell you how to prevent passing the virus to your sexual or needle sharing partners.

• You can increase your chances of staying healthy by eating a well-balanced, nutritious diet, getting enough sleep, exercising, avoiding alcohol, tobacco, and recreational drugs, reducing stress and having regular check-ups.

If you are a woman who receives an HIV positive test result:

• If you are thinking about having a child, your provider will give you information to help you make informed choices about your health care and pregnancy.

• If you are pregnant, your doctor can provide the care you need and information about services and options available to you. Your provider can tell you about the risks of passing HIV infection to your baby, about medications given during pregnancy that can significantly reduce the risk of passing HIV to your baby, and the medical care available for babies who may be infected with HIV.

• If you have given birth to or breast fed a child since you were infected, your child will need to be tested for HIV and, if infected, may need additional care and treatment. Your provider can give you information about medical care available for children who may be infected with HIV.

Confidentiality of HIV Information:

If you take the HIV antibody test, your test results are confidential. Under New York State law, confidential HIV information can only be given to people you allow to have it by giving your written approval, or to people who need to know your HIV status in order to provide medical care and services, including: medical care providers; persons involved with foster care or adoption; parents and guardians who consent to care of minors; jail, prison, probation and parole employees; emergency response workers and other workers in hospitals, other regulated settings or medical offices, who are exposed to blood/body fluids in the course of their employment; and organizations that review the services you receive. The law also allows your HIV information to be released under limited circumstances: by special court order; to public health officials as required by law; and to insurers as necessary to pay for care and treatment.

Reporting Requirements:

Your name will be reported to the health department if you have a confirmed positive HIV antibody test result received through a confidential test, other HIV-related test results, a diagnosis of AIDS, or if you have chosen to attach your name to a positive test result at an anonymous site. The health department will use this information to track the epidemic and to better plan prevention, health care and other services.

Notifying Partners:

If you test HIV positive, your provider will talk with you about the importance and benefits of notifying your partners of their possible exposure to HIV. It is important that your partners know they may have been exposed to HIV so they can find out whether they are infected and benefit from early diagnosis and treatment. Your provider may ask you to provide the names of your partners, and whether it is safe for you if they are notified. If you have been in an abusive relationship with one of these partners, it is important to share information with your provider. For information regarding services related to domestic violence, call 1-800-942-6906.

• Under state law, your provider is required to report to the health department the names of any of your partners (present and past sexual partners, including spouses, and needle sharing partners) whom they know.

• If you have additional partners whom your provider does not know, you may give their names to your provider so they can be notified.

• Several options are available to assist you and your provider in notifying partners. If you or your provider do not have a plan to notify your partners, the Health Department may notify them without revealing your identity. If this notification presents a risk of harm to you, the Health Department may defer the notification for a period of time sufficient to allow you to access domestic violence prevention services.

• If you do not name any partners to your provider or if a need exists to confirm information about your partners, the health department may contact you to request your cooperation in this process.

Confidentiality of HIV Test Results and Related Information:

If you feel your confidentiality has been broken, or for more information about HIV confidentiality, call the New York State Department of Health HIV Confidentiality Hotline at 1-800-962-5065. Any health or social service provider who illegally tells anyone about your HIV information may be punished by a fine of up to $5,000 and a jail term of up to one year. The law also protects you from HIV-related discrimination in housing, employment, health care or other services. For more information, call the New York State Division of Human Rights at 1-800-523-2437.

My questions about the HIV antibody test were answered. I agree to be tested for HIV.

Signature:	
Date:	

I provided pre-test counseling in accordance with Article 27-F of the New York State Public Health Law. I answered the above individual's questions about the test and offered him/her an unsigned copy of this form.

Signature: _____Title: _____

Facility/Provider Name: _____

APPENDIX 28:
TABLE OF STATE ANONYMITY/
CONFIDENTIALITY HIV TESTING
OPTIONS

STATE	TESTING OPTION
ALABAMA	Confidential Only
ALASKA	Anonymous and Confidential
ARIZONA	Anonymous and Confidential
ARKANSAS	Anonymous and Confidential
CALIFORNIA	Anonymous and Confidential
COLORADO	Anonymous and Confidential
CONNECTICUT	Anonymous and Confidential
DELAWARE	Anonymous and Confidential
DISTRICT OF COLUMBIA	Anonymous and Confidential
FLORIDA	Anonymous and Confidential
GEORGIA	Anonymous and Confidential
HAWAII	Anonymous and Confidential
IDAHO	Confidential Only
ILLINOIS	Anonymous and Confidential
INDIANA	Anonymous and Confidential
IOWA	Confidential Only
KANSAS	Anonymous and Confidential

STATE	TESTING OPTION
KENTUCKY	Anonymous and Confidential
LOUISIANA	Anonymous and Confidential
MAINE	Anonymous and Confidential
MARYLAND	Anonymous and Confidential
MASSACHUSETTS	Anonymous and Confidential
MICHIGAN	Anonymous and Confidential
MINNESOTA	Anonymous and Confidential
MISSISSIPPI	Confidential Only
MISSOURI	Anonymous and Confidential
MONTANA	Anonymous and Confidential
NEBRASKA	Anonymous and Confidential
NEVADA	Confidential Only
NEW HAMPSHIRE	Anonymous and Confidential
NEW JERSEY	Anonymous and Confidential
NEW MEXICO	Anonymous and Confidential
NEW YORK	Anonymous and Confidential
NORTH CAROLINA	Confidential Only
NORTH DAKOTA	Confidential Only
OHIO	Anonymous and Confidential
OKLAHOMA	Anonymous and Confidential
OREGON	Anonymous and Confidential
PENNSYLVANIA	Anonymous and Confidential
RHODE ISLAND	Anonymous and Confidential
SOUTH CAROLINA	Confidential Only
SOUTH DAKOTA	Confidential Only
TENNESSEE	Confidential Only
TEXAS	Anonymous and Confidential
UTAH	Anonymous and Confidential
VERMONT	Anonymous and Confidential

STATE	TESTING OPTION
VIRGINIA	Anonymous and Confidential
WASHINGTON	Anonymous and Confidential
WEST VIRGINIA	Anonymous and Confidential
WISCONSIN	Anonymous and Confidential
WYOMING	Anonymous and Confidential

Source: Centers for Disease Control and Prevention (May 2007)

APPENDIX 29: INFORMED CONSENT TO PERFORM AN EXPEDITED HIV TEST IN THE DELIVERY SETTING

Informed Consent to Perform an Expedited HIV Test in the Delivery Setting
New York State Department of Health

HIV testing is voluntary and requires your consent in writing. The purpose of expedited HIV testing is to show if you are infected with HIV, the virus that causes AIDS. If you are HIV-infected, expedited HIV testing will allow you to receive immediate medication during labor and delivery to reduce the risk of transmitting HIV to your newborn, and will allow your baby to receive the same medication immediately after birth.

Before you consent to be tested for HIV, speak to your health care provider about: How HIV can be passed from person to person and mother to baby;

The medication that has been shown in many cases to prevent the transmission of HIV from mother to baby; The New York State law that requires all newborns to be tested for HIV after birth (without the parents' consent); and,
The meaning of preliminary HIV test results and how a positive HIV test will be confirmed.

If you agree with the following statements and want to consent to expedited HIV testing, please sign on the other side of this form.

I have been counseled about the benefits of having an expedited HIV test and I understand that HIV infection can be passed from mother to baby.

I understand that:

• The human immunodeficiency virus (HIV) is the virus that causes AIDS.

• One of the ways that HIV is spread is by sexual intercourse, so all pregnant women are potentially at risk for HIV infection.

• HIV can be passed from a mother to her baby during pregnancy, at delivery, and through breastfeeding.

• If I have HIV, it is a serious illness that can affect my health and the health of my baby.

• HIV antibody test results are confidential and the law protects me from discrimination related to HIV.

If I am found to be HIV-infected, treatment is available to reduce the risk that my baby will be infected:

• If I have not yet delivered my baby, I may receive medication as soon as possible which may greatly reduce the chance of my passing the virus to my baby.

• My baby may receive medication which reduces the risk of his/her becoming HIV-infected.

• If medication to reduce the risk of transmission of HIV is given to me during labor and delivery, or to my newborn immediately after birth, the chance that my baby will be HIV-infected is about 1 in 12. Without treatment, the chance that my baby will be infected is about 1 in 4.

• If treatment is started, my health care provider will discuss any consequences of taking the medication with me.

INFORMED CONSENT TO PERFORM AN EXPEDITED HIV TEST

New York State has a Newborn Screening Program:

• If I do not consent to expedited testing now, my baby will be tested for HIV without consent immediately after birth.

• All babies born in New York State are also routinely tested for HIV as a part of the Newborn Screening Program; the test results are reported to their mothers.

The test I am consenting to take will provide me and my health care provider with results within 48 hours:

• If I have the expedited HIV test, I will be given the results no later than 48 hours after my blood is drawn.

• If the expedited HIV test result is negative, no further testing will be done at this time.

• If my expedited HIV test result is negative, it most likely means that I am not infected with HIV, but it may not show recent infection.

• A positive preliminary HIV test result means that there is a possibility that I am HIV-infected and that my baby may have been exposed to HIV. A second test, to confirm a preliminary positive HIV test result, will be done.

• I understand that if my preliminary test result is positive, I still may not have HIV infection (false positive tests can occur) but that it may be best to start treatment to help prevent the transmission of infection to my baby while I wait for the confirmatory test result.

• If my preliminary HIV test result is positive, my health care provider will advise me not to begin breastfeeding until the confirmatory test is done.

All preliminary positive test results will be confirmed:

• If the confirmatory HIV test result is negative, both my baby and I will immediately be taken off medication if it was started to help prevent transmission of HIV from me to my baby.

• If the confirmatory test is positive, any medication that was begun to help prevent transmission of HIV from me to my baby will be continued.

• If my confirmatory test is positive, further testing will be needed to determine whether or not my baby has HIV infection.

• If the confirmatory test is positive, I will be referred to a physician for my own ongoing medical care and I will be referred to a health care provider who will take care of my baby's medical needs.

Confidentiality of HIV Information:

If you take the HIV antibody test, your test results are confidential. Under New York State law, confidential HIV information can only be given to people you allow to have it by giving your written approval, or to people who need to know your HIV status in order to provide medical care and services, including: medical care providers; persons involved with foster care or adoption; parents and guardians who consent to care of minors; jail, prison, probation and parole employees; emergency response workers and other workers in hospitals, other regulated settings or medical offices, who are exposed to blood/body fluids in the course of their employment; and organizations that review the services you receive. The law also allows your HIV information to be released under certain limited circumstances: by special court order; to public health officials as required by law; and to insurers as necessary to pay for care and treatment.

Reporting Requirements:

Your name will be reported to the Health Department if you have a confirmed positive HIV antibody test result received through a confidential test, other HIV-related test results, a diagnosis of AIDS, or if you have chosen to attach your name to a positive test result at an anonymous site. The Health Department will use this information to track the epidemic and to better plan prevention, health care and other services.

Notifying Partners:

If you test HIV positive, your provider will talk with you about the importance and benefits of notifying your partners of their possible exposure to HIV. It is important that your partners know they may have been exposed to HIV so they can find out whether they are infected and benefit from early diagnosis and treatment. Your provider may ask you to provide the names of your partners, and whether it is safe for you if they are notified. If you have been in an abusive relationship with one of these partners, it is important to share information with your provider. For information regarding services related to domestic violence, call 1-800-942-6906.

	Under state law, your provider is required to report to the Health Department the names of any of your partners (present and past sexual partners, including spouses, and needle sharing partners) whom they know.
	If you have additional partners whom your provider does not know, you may give their names to your provider so they can be notified.
	Several options are available to assist you and your provider in notifying partners. If you or your provider do not have a plan to notify your partners, the Health Department may notify them without revealing your identity. If this notification presents a risk to you, the Health Department may defer the notification for a period of time sufficient to allow you to access domestic violence prevention services.
	If you do not name any partners to your provider or if a need exists to confirm information about your partners, the Health Department may contact you to request your cooperation in this process.

Confidentiality of HIV Test Results and Related Information:

If you feel your confidentiality has been broken, or for more information about HIV confidentiality, call the New York State Department of Health HIV Confidentiality Hotline at 1-800-962-5065. Any health or social service provider who illegally tells anyone about your HIV information may be punished by a fine of up to $5,000 and a jail term of up to one year. The law also protects you from HIV-related discrimination in housing, employment, health care or other services. For more information, call the New York State Division of Human Rights at 1-800-523-2437.

My questions about the HIV antibody test were answered. I agree to be tested for HIV.

Signature: _____ Date: _____

I provided pre-test counseling in accordance with Article 27-F of the New York State Public Health Law. I answered the above individual's questions about the test and offered her an unsigned copy of this form.

Signature: _____ Title: _____

Facility/Provider Name: _____

APPENDIX 30:
TABLE OF STATE STATUTES CONCERNING HIV PARTNER NOTIFICATION

STATE	STATUTE	SUMMARY
ALABAMA	Ala. Code §22-11A-38(d)	Physicians or the state health official may notify a third party where there is a "foreseeable, real or probably risk of transmission of the disease."
ALABAMA	Ala. Code §22-11A-38(f)	Extends immunity from liability to physicians, health department employees, and hospitals and other health care facilities, for notifying or failing to notify partners exposed to infected person.
ALABAMA	Ala. Code §22-11A-53	Notification of positive HIV test result shall include an explanation of the benefits of locating, testing and counseling partners and a full description of the public health services for locating and counseling partners.
ARIZONA	Ariz. Rev. Stat §32-1457(A/§32-1860(A)	A physician may report the name of the spouse or sex/needlesharing partner of a patient that has tested positive for HIV to the department of health services if: the physician knows that the patient has not or will not notify these people; and

STATE	STATUTE	SUMMARY
		the physician has asked the patient to release this information voluntarily.
ARIZONA	Ariz. Rev. Stat. §32-1457(C)/§32-1860(C)	Extends immunity from liability to physicians for notifying or failing to notify partners exposed to infected person.
ARIZONA	Ariz. Rev. Stat. §36-664(K)	Any person who knows that an individual is HIV positive, and who reasonably believes that an identifiable third party is at risk of HIV infection from that individual, may report that risk to the Health Department. Upon receipt of such report the department shall notify the person at risk.
ARIZONA	Ariz. Rev. Stat. §36-665	Any person who knows that an individual is HIV positive, and who reasonably believes that an identifiable third party is at risk of HIV infection from that individual, may report that risk to the Health Department. Upon receipt of such report the department shall notify the person at risk.
ARIZONA	Ariz. Rev. Stat §36-666(C)	Extends immunity from civil or criminal liability to a health care facility or health care provider for failing to notify the contact of a person with a communicable disease.
CALIFORNIA	Cal. Health & Safety Code §121015	A physician may notify a person reasonably believed to be the spouse or sex/needle-sharing partner of a patient testing positive for HIV of their exposure to HIV if the physician has: discussed the test results with the patient and offered appropriate educational and psychological counseling; and notified the patient of the intent to notify patient's partners prior to notification. A physician has no duty to notify and may not be held criminally or civilly liable for

TABLE OF STATE STATUTES—HIV PARTNER NOTIFICATION

STATE	STATUTE	SUMMARY
		notifying partners. A physician may also report risk of exposure to third parties to the health department, which may then alert those persons to their risk.
COLORADO	Col. Rev. Stat. §25-4-1405.5 (2)(a)(II)	The state board of health shall adopt rules specifying the performance standards for anonymous and confidential counseling and testing, including standards for partner notification.
COLORADO	Col. Rev. Stat. §25-4-1406	As a last resort, the executive director of the state department of public health, or the director of the local department of health may issue an order to direct a person with HIV infection to cease and desist from specified conduct which endangers the health of others.
CONNECTICUT	Conn. Gen, Stat. §19a-584(a)	A public health officer may notify the partner of a person infected with HIV if: (1) she reasonably believes a significant risk of transmission exists; (2) she reasonably believes that the index patient will not himself warn the contact; and (3) she has informed the patient of her intent to warn the third party. The physician or public health officer has no obligation to warn, inform, identify or locate any partner.
CONNECTICUT	Conn. Gen. Stat. §19a-584(b)	A physician may notify a known partner of a patient who tests positive for HIV, if that partner is also a patient of the physician. A physician must follow the same procedures as public health officers before notifying a partner.
CONNECTICUT	Conn. Gen. Stat. §19a-582(b)	Anyone taking a test for HIV must be told before the test that if they test positive, public health counselors or a physician may notify their known partners of a risk of infection whether or not they have consent to do so.

AIDS Law

163

STATE	STATUTE	SUMMARY
DELAWARE	Del. Code §16-1203(a)(10)	Allowing disclosure of HIV test results to a third party on court order based on "compelling need."
DELAWARE	Del. Code §16-1205(c)	Extends immunity from civil or criminal liability for disclosure of an HIV test result under §1203.
DISTRICT OF COLUMBIA	D.C. Code §6-117	A court may order disclosure of HIV status to a third person if it finds, upon clear and convincing evidence, that it is essential to safeguard the physical health of others. The person whose status is to be disclosed shall have an opportunity to contest the disclosure.
FLORIDA	Fl. Stat. §381.004(3)(e)	No HIV test result shall be revealed to the test subject without telling the subject the benefits of locating and counseling any individual that may have been exposed to HIV by the subject and of the availability of public health services to help locate and counsel partners.
FLORIDA	Fl. Stat. §381.004(3)(f)(9)	A court may order HIV test results disclosed to a third party on a showing of compelling need, and after weighing the privacy interest of the test subject and the public interest which may be disserved by disclosure which deters HIV testing or which may lead to discrimination.
FLORIDA	Fl. Stat. §381.004(4)(c)	Each county health department shall provide counseling and testing on an anonymous basis, including informing clients of the availability of partner notification services and the benefits of such services.
FLORIDA	Fl. Stat.§384.26	Permitting the health department to interview all HIV positive individuals for information regarding the identification and notification of partners.

STATE	STATUTE	SUMMARY
FLORIDA	Fl. Stat. §455.674	A health practitioner shall not be civilly or criminally liable for disclosing confidential HIV information to a sex or needle-sharing partner of a patient testing positive for HIV if the practitioner first recommends that the patient notify the partner or refrain from risk activities, and the practitioner has told the patient of her intent to inform the partner. A practitioner is not liable for failing to disclose such information.
GEORGIA	Ga. Code §24-9-47(g)	A physician may notify a spouse, sexual partner or child of a patient infected with HIV that the physician reasonably believes to be at risk of exposure. The physician must attempt to notify the patient that disclosure will be made.
GEORGIA	Ga. Code §24-9-47(h)(3)(B)	The Department of Human Resources may contact any person reasonably believed to be at risk of being infected with HIV to disclose their possible exposure to HIV.
GEORGIA	Ga. Code §24-9-47(h)(3)(C)	The Department of Human Resources must contact and inform the spouse of an HIV infected person of their exposure if they are reasonably likely to have engaged in risk activities with the infected person.
GEORGIA	Ga. Code §24-9-47(j)	Extends immunity from civil or criminal liability for authorized disclosure to third parties. Releases persons authorized to make disclosures from duty to disclose or liability for failing to disclose exposure to HIV to third parties.
HAWAII	Haw. Code §325-10(a)(4)	Physicians and public health officers may notify sex or needle-sharing partners of an HIV positive patient where: (1) there is reason to believe that the contact is at risk of HIV transmission; and (2) the patient has

STATE	STATUTE	SUMMARY
		been counseled and is unwilling to inform the contact directly or consent to disclosure by a third person. Physicians and public health officers have no obligation to identify or locate any contact and are immune from civil or criminal liability.
IDAHO	Idaho Code §39-610(2)	State or local health authorities may contact and advise people who authorities believe to have been exposed to HIV.
IDAHO	Idaho Code §39-610(5)	Extends immunity for civil or criminal liability for authorized disclosure or for nondisclosure.
ILLINOIS	Ill. Comp. Stat. §410-205-9	A physician may notify the spouse of a patient who tests positive for HIV if the physician has tried to persuade the patient to notify the spouse or if, after a patient has agreed to make the notification the physician has reason to believe that the patient has not provided the notification. This section does not create a duty or obligation for a physician to notify the spouse, and no civil or criminal liability may be imposed on the physician for disclosing or failing to disclose HIV test results to a spouse.
ILLINOIS	Ill. Comp. Stat. §410-325-5.5	When the department of public health determines that a person infected with HIV may be exposing others to HIV, the department shall investigate the person with HIV and her contacts and notify the contacts if it appears that the person with HIV will not carry out notification.
INDIANA	Ind. Stat. §16-41-7-1	A person who is infected with HIV has a duty to warn or cause to be warned by a third party people with whom they are engaged in activities that carry a high risk of transmission of HIV.

STATE	STATUTE	SUMMARY
INDIANA	Ind. Stat. §16-41-7-3(a)	A physician must inform patients with HIV of their duty to notify partners.
INDIANA	Ind. Stat. §16-41-7-3(b)(1)	A physician may notify a health officer of patients with HIV that pose a serious and present danger to the health of others, patients suspected of being at risk, or any other person reasonably believed to be at risk of contracting HIV.
INDIANA	Ind. Stat. §16-41-7-3(b)(2)	A physician may also notify persons at risk directly if she has reason to believe that they have been exposed to HIV, that they will not be informed by any other person, and she has made reasonable efforts to inform the patient of her intent to notify the person at risk.
INDIANA	Ind. Stat. §16-41-7-3(d)	A physician who provides notification in good faith is immune from civil or criminal liability.
INDIANA	Ind. Stat. §16-41-7-4	A health officer or the state department shall notify persons reported to be at risk unless they determine that intervention is not necessary.
IOWA	Iowa Code §141.6(3)(a)	Department of public health shall provide for a person who tests positive for HIV to receive counseling and be encouraged to refer partners for notification.
IOWA	Iowa Code §141.6(3)(d)(2)	When a physician believes that a patient infected with HIV will not warn a third party at risk, and will not participate in the voluntary partner notification program, she may reveal the identity of the patient to the extent necessary to protect the party at risk. The physician shall attempt to notify the infected patient of her intent to notify, the person to be notified,

STATE	STATUTE	SUMMARY
		and the anticipated date of disclosure.
KANSAS	Kan. Stat. §65-6004	A physician who has reason to believe that the spouse or partner of a person who has tested positive for HIV has been exposed to HIV and is unaware of their exposure, may inform them of their risk of exposure. Such disclosure is immune from civil or criminal liability, and no duty to warn is created.
LOUISIANA	La. Stat. §1300.14(E)	A physician may notify contacts of a patient infected with HIV if: she reasonably believes there is a significant risk of transmission to the contact; if the patient has been counseled and the physician reasonably believes that the patient will not inform the contact; and the physician has informed the patient of her intent to notify the contact. The physician has no obligation to identify or locate any contact.
LOUISIANA	La. Stat. §1300.15	A court may grant an order for disclosure of HIV test results to a third person upon a showing of a "clear and imminent danger to an individual whose life or health may unknowingly be at significant risk" as a result of contact with an individual whose HIV status is sought. "The court shall weigh the need for disclosure against the privacy interest of the protected individual and against the public interest that may not be served by disclosure which deters future testing or treatment or which may lead to discrimination."
MAINE	Me. Rev. Stat. §19203-D(A)	HIV infection status may be released only if the person to whom the information pertains has specifically authorized a separate release of that information. A general release form is insufficient.

STATE	STATUTE	SUMMARY
MAINE	Me. Rev. Stat. §801	A person who fails or refuses to cooperate with a health department contact notification program, or who engages in behavior that creates a significant risk of transmission of a communicable disease is considered a "public health threat."
MAINE	Me. Rev. Stat. §808	A public health department investigative team shall have access to medical and laboratory records relevant to the investigation of a public health threat.
MAINE	Me. Rev. Stat. §810	Upon a showing of clear and convincing evidence that a person requires immediate custody in order to avoid a clear and immediate public health threat, a judge of the district court may grant temporary custody of the person and may order specific emergency care, treatment or evaluation.
MARYLAND	Md. Health Gen. Code §18-336(b)(2)	Counseling before HIV testing must include informing the test subject of the physician's duty to warn third parties who may be at risk of contracting HIV from the subject.
MARYLAND	Md. Health Gen. Code §18-337(b)	If an individual tests positive for HIV and refuses to notify her sex/needlesharing partners, the individual's physician may inform the local health officer and/or the individual's partners directly, of the identity of the HIV-positive patient and the circumstances giving rise to the notification. A physician may not be held liable for disclosure or nondisclosure if acting in good faith.
MICHIGAN	Mich. Stat. Ann. §14.15(5131)(5)(b)	Creates an affirmative duty for a physician or local health officer to notify known partners of individuals infected with HIV or diagnosed as having AIDS, if the

STATE	STATUTE	SUMMARY
		physical or health officer determines that notification is necessary to prevent a reasonably foreseeable risk of transmission of HIV.
MICHIGAN	Mich. Stat. Ann. §14.15(5131)(6)	A person who releases information in the course of partner notification is immune from civil or criminal liability.
MICHIGAN	Mich. Stat. Ann. §14.15(5131)(7)	A person who notifies a partner of an HIV infected individual shall not include information that identifies the infected individual unless the identifying information is determined by the person making the disclosure to be reasonably necessary to prevent a foreseeable risk of transmission of HIV.
MICHIGAN	Mich. Stat. Ann. §14.15(5114a)(1)	A person or government entity that administers a test for HIV shall refer individuals testing positive for assistance with partner notification if they determine that the individual needs assistance with partner notification
MICHIGAN	Mich. Stat. Ann. §14.15(5114a)(3)	A local health department that assists individuals with partner notification must inform the individual that he has a legal obligation to inform each of his sexual partners of his infection before engaging in sexual relations with that partner, and that he may be subject to criminal sanctions for failure to so inform his partners.
MICHIGAN	Mich. Stat. Ann. §14.15(5114a)(5)	If a local health department receives a report that indicates that a resident of the state is HIV infected, the health department shall make it a priority to attempt to interview the individual and offer to contact the individual's sex/needle-sharing partners, and within 35 days of interview to contact each individual identified as a partner.

STATE	STATUTE	SUMMARY
MISSOURI	Mo. Rev. Stat. §191.656(2)(1)(d)	Unless a person acts in bad faith or with conscious disregard, no person will be liable for violating any duty or right of confidentiality for disclosing the results of an individual's HIV testing to the spouse of the subject of the test.
MISSOURI	Mo. Rev. Stat. §191.656(2)(2)	Paragraph (d) does not impose any duty to disclose HIV testing results.
MISSOURI	Mo. Rev. Stat. §191.656(6)	A person who negligently violates this section is liable for actual damages, injunctive relief, court costs and reasonable attorney's fees, and a person who willfully or intentionally or recklessly violates this section is liable for the same damages and for exemplary damages.
MISSOURI	Mo. Rev. Stat. §191.686(4)	All anonymous test sites are required to initiate partner notification when submitting test results to individuals who test positive for HIV.
MONTANA	Mont. Code Ann. §50-16-1009(3)	A health care provider shall encourage a subject testing positive for HIV to notify potential contacts. If the subject is unable or unwilling to notify contacts, the health care provider may ask the subject to disclose voluntarily the identities of the contacts and to authorize notification of the contacts by a health care provider.
MONTANA	Mont. Code Ann. §50-16-529(9)	A health care provider may disclose health care information about a patient, without the patient's authorization, to any contact if the health care provider reasonably believes that disclosure will avoid or minimize an imminent danger to the health or safety of the contact or any other individual.

STATE	STATUTE	SUMMARY
MONTANA	Mont. Code Ann. §50-16-1004	Expressing the intent of the legislature to treat AIDS and HIV infection in the same manner as other communicable diseases, including sexually transmitted diseases, by adopting the most currently accepted public health practices with regard to, among other things, partner notification.
MONTANA	Mont. Code Ann. §50-18-106	If a physician or other person knows or has reason to suspect that a person who has a sexually transmitted disease is conducting himself in a way which might expose another to infection, he shall immediately notify the local health officer of the name and address of the diseased person and the essential facts in the case.
NEBRASKA	Neb. Rev. Stat. §71-501.02(6)	To the extent funds are available, the Department of Health and Human Services may offer partner notification services that are culturally and language specific upon request to persons testing positive for HIV.
NEVADA	Nev. Rev. Stat. Ann. §441A.220(5)	Confidential information about a communicable disease may be disclosed to any person who has a medical need to know the information for his own protection or for the well-being of a patient or dependent person.
NEW JERSEY	N.J. Stat. §26:5C-9(a)	The record of a person who has or is suspected of having AIDS or HIV infection may be disclosed by an order of a court upon a showing of good cause. At a good cause hearing the court shall weigh the public interest and need for disclosure against injury to the person who is the subject of the record, to the physician-patient relationship, and to the services offered by the program.

STATE	STATUTE	SUMMARY
NEW MEXICO	N.M. Stat. Ann. §24-1-8	If a physician knows or has good reason to suspect that a person with an STD may conduct himself so as to expose other persons to infection, he shall notify the district health officer of the name and address of the diseased person and the facts of the case.
NEW MEXICO	N.M. Stat. Ann. §24-2B-4	A person who tests positive for HIV must be informed of the benefits of locating and counseling any partners that may have been exposed to HIV.
NEW YORK	N.Y. Pub. Health Law §2782(4)(a)	A physician may disclose confidential HIV-related information to a contact or to a public health officer for disclosure to a contact if: the physician reasonably believes there is a significant risk of infection to the contact; the physician has counseled the patient infected with HIV of the need to notify the contact; the physician reasonably believes the patient will not inform the contact; and the physician has informed the patient of her intent to notify the contact.
NEW YORK	N.Y. Pub. Health Law §2782(4)(c)	A physician or public health officer has no obligation to identify or locate any contact.
NEW YORK	N.Y. Pub. Health Law §2785(5)	In assessing compelling need and clear and imminent danger, the court shall weigh the need for disclosure against the privacy interest of the protected individual and the public interest which may be disserved by disclosure which deters future testing or treatment or which may lead to discrimination.
NEW YORK	N.Y. Pub. Health Law §2785(2)(b)	A court may grant an order for disclosure of confidential HIV-related information upon a

STATE	STATUTE	SUMMARY
		showing of clear and imminent danger to an individual whose life or health may unknowingly be at significant risk as a result of contact with the individual to whom the information pertains.
NORTH CAROLINA	N.C. Gen. Stat. §130A-143(4)	Information relating to the HIV status of an individual may be released if necessary to protect the public health and is made as provided by the Commission in its rules regarding control measures for communicable diseases.
NORTH DAKOTA	N.D. Cent. Code §23-07.4-01(2)(c)	When a state health officer knows, or has reason to believe that a person has HIV and is a danger to the public health, and the infected person has been ordered to report for counseling and information on how to avoid infecting others, that official may issue an order to direct that person to cease and desist from specified conduct that endangers the health of others.
NORTH DAKOTA	N.D. Cent. Code §23-07.4-01(4)	If a court affirms the order, and the person subject to the order is infected with HIV, the court shall require the person to disclose the names and addresses of sex/needle-sharing partners. Failure to comply with court-ordered disclosure constitutes contempt of court.
NORTH DAKOTA	N.D. Cent. Code §23-07.4-02	If the procedures of the previous section have been exhausted, and a person believed to be infected with HIV continues to engage in behavior that presents an imminent danger to the public health, a court may issue other orders, including an order to take the person into custody, for a period not to exceed 90 days and place the person in a facility designated or approved by the state health officer.

STATE	STATUTE	SUMMARY
OHIO	Ohio Rev. Code Ann. §3701.241(A)	The director of public health shall develop and administer both confidential and anonymous tests for HIV and a confidential partner notification system.
OHIO	Ohio Rev. Code Ann. §3701-241(B)	The director shall prepare a list of sites where an individual may obtain an anonymous HIV test, and make available a copy of the list to anyone who requests it.
OHIO	Ohio Rev. Code Ann. §3701.243(C)(1)(b)	A court may issue an order granting access to or authority to disclose HIV test results only if the court finds by clear and convincing evidence that there is a compelling need for disclosure. The court shall weigh the need for disclosure against the privacy right of the individual tested and against any disservice to the public interest that might result from the disclosure, such as discrimination against the individual or the deterrence of others from being tested.
OHIO	Ohio Rev. Code Ann. §3701.243(F)	An individual who knows that he is HIV positive shall disclose this information to any other person with whom he intends to have sex or share a hypodermic needle.
OKLAHOMA	Okla. Stat. §1-502.2	Confidential information about a person with a communicable disease may be released if necessary to protect the health and well-being of the general public.
OREGON	Ore. Rev. Stat. §433.008	If the local public health administrator determines that a person with a contagious disease is violating the rules of the division pertaining to control of that disease, it may disclose that

STATE	STATUTE	SUMMARY
		person's name and address to a third person if clear and convincing evidence requires disclosure to avoid a clear and immediate danger to other individuals or to the public generally. A decision not to disclose information, if made in good faith, shall not subject the person withholding the information to liability.
PENNSYLVANIA	Pa. Stat. §7609(A)	), a physician may disclose confidential HIV-related information to a known contact of a patient infected with HIV if: the physician reasonably believes disclosure is medically appropriate and there is a significant risk of future infection to the contact; the physician has counseled the patient about the need to notify the contact and the physician reasonably believes the patient will not inform the contact or abstain from activities which pose a significant risk of infection to the contact.
PENNSYLVANIA	Pa. Stat. §7609(B)	A physician shall have no duty to identify, locate or notify any contact and no cause of action shall arise for nondisclosure or for disclosure.
PENNSYLVANIA	Pa. Stat. §7608	A court may issue an order to allow access to confidential HIV related information upon a showing of compelling need.
RHODE ISLAND	R. I. Gen. Laws §23-6-17(2)(v)	A physician may disclose the HIV-positive status of a patient to a third party who has contact with that patient if there is a clear and present danger of HIV transmission to the third party, and if, despite the physician's strong encouragement, the patient has not and will not warn the third party.

STATE	STATUTE	SUMMARY
SOUTH CAROLINA	S.C. Stat. Ann. §44-29-146	A physician or state agency identifying and notifying a spouse or known contact of a person having HIV is not liable for damages resulting from the disclosure.
SOUTH CAROLINA	S.C. Stat. Ann. §44-29-90	The Department of Health and Environmental Control must, to the extent resources are available, notify known sex/needle-sharing contacts of a person who has HIV.
SOUTH DAKOTA	S.D. Codified Laws §34-22-9(3)	The department of health shall establish procedures for communicable disease contact notification, referral and management.
SOUTH DAKOTA	S.D. Codified Laws §34-22-12.1	Confidential information about a communicable disease may be disclosed to the extent necessary to protect the health or life of a named person.
TENNESSEE	Tenn. Code Ann. §68-5-101	Whenever any case of communicable disease exists or is suspected to exist in any household, it is the duty of the head of the household, or any other person in the household possessing knowledge of the facts, to notify the municipal or county health authorities.
TENNESSEE	Tenn. Code Ann. §68-10-115	A person who has a reasonable belief that a person has knowingly exposed another to HIV may inform the potential victim without incurring any liability.
TEXAS	Tex. Health & Safety Code §81-051(g)(1)	A partner notification program shall notify the partner of a person with HIV infection with or without the consent of the person with HIV.

STATE	STATUTE	SUMMARY
TEXAS	Tex. Health & Safety Code §81-051(g)(2)	A health care professional shall notify the partner notification program when the health care professional knows the HIV status of a patient and has actual knowledge of possible transmission of HIV to a third party.
TEXAS	Tex. Health & Safety Code §81-051(h)	A health care professional who fails to make the notification required by section (g) is immune from civil or criminal liability.
UTAH	Utah Code Ann. §26-63.5	The department of health shall utilize contact tracing and other methods for partner identification and notification.
VIRGINIA	Va. Code Ann. §32.1-36.1	The results of a test for HIV may be released to the spouse of the person tested.
VIRGINIA	Va. Code Ann. §32.1-37.2	Every person who tests for HIV shall be informed of the need to notify any partners who may have been exposed to the virus.
WASHINGTON	Wash. Rev. Code §70.24.105(f)	A court may order disclosure of an HIV test to a third party on a showing of good cause and weighing the public interest and the need for disclosure against the injury to the patient, to the physician patient relationship, and to the treatment services.
WASHINGTON	Wash. Rev. Code §70.24.105(h)	If a health officer determines that a person has been placed at risk of contracting HIV, and that the exposed person is unaware of the risk, then the identity of the person with HIV that they are in contact with may be disclosed.
WEST VIRGINIA	W. Va. Code §16-3C-3(d)	Sex or needle-sharing partners of a person with HIV may be notified of their exposure to HIV without revealing the identity of the person with HIV, and no cause of action may arise from such notification.

STATE	STATUTE	SUMMARY
WEST VIRGINIA	W. Va. Code §16-3C-3(e)	A physician or health care provider has no duty to notify the spouse or other sex or needle-sharing partner of a person infected with HIV, and no cause of action may arise from the failure to notify.
WISCONSIN	Wisc. Stat. §252.12	The public health department shall contact individuals who test positive for HIV and encourage them to refer any sex or needle-sharing partners for counseling and testing.
WYOMING	Wyo. Stat. §35-4-133	A health officer shall make every reasonable effort to notify any sex or needlesharing partners of a person with a sexually transmitted disease (including HIV) of their possible exposure to infection.

Source: American Civil Liberties Union (ACLU)

APPENDIX 31:
TABLE OF STATE NAME
REPORTING REQUIREMENTS

STATE	HIV REPORTING REQUIREMENT	DATE NAME REPORTING REQUIREMENT INITIATED
ALABAMA	Name	January 1998
ALASKA	Name	February 1999
ARIZONA	Name	January 1987
ARKANSAS	Name	July 1989
CALIFORNIA	Name	April 2006
COLORADO	Name	November 1985
CONNECTICUT	Name	January 2005
DELAWARE	Name	February 2006
DISTRICT OF COLUMBIA	Name	November 2006
FLORIDA	Name	July 1997
GEORGIA	Name	December 2003
HAWAII	Code	N/A
IDAHO	Name	June 1986
ILLINOIS	Name	January 2006
INDIANA	Name	July 1988
IOWA	Name	July 1998
KANSAS	Name	July 1999

STATE	HIV REPORTING REQUIREMENT	DATE NAME REPORTING REQUIREMENT INITIATED
KENTUCKY	Name	October 2004
LOUISIANA	Name	February 1993
MAINE	Name	January 2006
MARYLAND	Name	April 2007
MASSACHUSETTS	Name	January 2007
MICHIGAN	Name	April 1992
MINNESOTA	Name	October 1985
MISSISSIPPI	Name	August 1988
MISSOURI	Name	October 1987
MONTANA	Name	September 2006
NEBRASKA	Name	September 1995
NEVADA	Name	February 1992
NEW HAMPSHIRE	Name	January 2005
NEW JERSEY	Name	January 1992
NEW MEXICO	Name	January 1998
NEW YORK	Name	June 2000
NORTH CAROLINA	Name	February 1990
NORTH DAKOTA	Name	January 1988
OHIO	Name	June 1990
OKLAHOMA	Name	June 1988
OREGON	Name	April 2006
PENNSYLVANIA	Name	October 2002
RHODE ISLAND	Name	July 2006
SOUTH CAROLINA	Name	February 1986
SOUTH DAKOTA	Name	January 1988
TENNESSEE	Name	January 1992
TEXAS	Name	January 1999
UTAH	Name	April 1989

STATE	HIV REPORTING REQUIREMENT	DATE NAME REPORTING REQUIREMENT INITIATED
VERMONT	Code	N/A
VIRGINIA	Name	July 1989
WASHINGTON	Name	March 2006
WEST VIRGINIA	Name	January 1989
WISCONSIN	Name	November 1985
WYOMING	Name	June 1989

Source: Centers for Disease Control and Prevention (May 2007)

APPENDIX 32:
SAMPLE AUTHORIZATION FOR RELEASE OF HEALTH INFORMATION PURSUANT TO THE HIPAA PRIVACY RULE (OCA FORM No: 960)

AUTHORIZATION FOR RELEASE OF HEALTH INFORMATION PURSUANT TO HIPAA
[This form has been approved by the New York State Department of Health]

Patient Name	Date of Birth	Social Security Number

Patient Address

I, or my authorized representative, request that health information regarding my care and treatment be released as set forth on this form:

In accordance with New York State Law and the Privacy Rule of the Health Insurance Portability and Accountability Act of 1996 (HIPAA), I understand that:

1. This authorization may include disclosure of information relating to **ALCOHOL** and **DRUG ABUSE, MENTAL HEALTH TREATMENT**, except psychotherapy notes, and **CONFIDENTIAL HIV* RELATED INFORMATION** only if I place my initials on the appropriate line in Item 9(a). In the event the health information described below includes any of these types of information, and I initial the line on the box in Item 9(a), I specifically authorize release of such information to the person(s) indicated in Item 8.

2. If I am authorizing the release of HIV-related, alcohol or drug treatment, or mental health treatment information, the recipient is prohibited from redisclosing such information without my authorization unless permitted to do so under federal or state law. I understand that I have the right to request a list of people who may receive or use my HIV-related information without authorization. If I experience discrimination because of the release or disclosure of HIV-related information, I may contact the New York State Division of Human Rights at (212) 480-2493 or the New York City Commission of Human Rights at (212) 306-7450. These agencies are responsible for protecting my rights.

3. I have the right to revoke this authorization at any time by writing to the health care provider listed below. I understand that I may revoke this authorization except to the extent that action has already been taken based on this authorization.

4. I understand that signing this authorization is voluntary. My treatment, payment, enrollment in a health plan, or eligibility for benefits will not be conditioned upon my authorization of this disclosure.

5. Information disclosed under this authorization might be redisclosed by the recipient (except as noted above in Item 2), and this redisclosure may no longer be protected by federal or state law.

SAMPLE AUTHORIZATION FOR RELEASE OF HEALTH INFORMATION

6. THIS AUTHORIZATION DOES NOT AUTHORIZE YOU TO DISCUSS MY HEALTH INFORMATION OR MEDICAL CARE WITH ANYONE OTHER THAN THE ATTORNEY OR GOVERNMENTAL AGENCY SPECIFIED IN ITEM 9 (b).

7. Name and address of health provider or entity to release this information:

8. Name and address of person(s) or category of person to whom this information will be sent:

9(a). Specific information to be released:
❏ Medical Record from (insert date) _____ to (insert date) _____
❏ Entire Medical Record, including patient histories, office notes (except psychotherapy notes), test results, radiology studies, films, referrals, consults, billing records, insurance records, and records sent to you by other health care providers.
❏ Other: _____   Include: (*Indicate by Initialing*)
_____   _____ **Alcohol/Drug Treatment**
                                                                _____ **Mental Health Information**
Authorization to Discuss Health Information   _____ **HIV-Related Information**

(b) ❏ By initialing here _____ I authorize _____
                           Initials   Name of individual health care provider
to discuss my health information with my attorney, or a governmental agency, listed here:

_____
(Attorney/Firm Name or Governmental Agency Name)

10. Reason for release of information: ❏ At request of individual ❏ Other:	11. Date or event on which this authorization will expire:
12. If not the patient, name of person signing form:	13. Authority to sign on behalf of patient:

All items on this form have been completed and my questions about this form have been answered. In addition, I have been provided a copy of the form.

Date: _____

_____
Signature of patient or representative authorized by law.

* **Human Immunodeficiency Virus that causes AIDS. The New York State Public Health Law protects information which reasonably could identify someone as having HIV symptoms or infection and information regarding a person's contacts.**

Instructions for the Use

of the HIPAA-compliant Authorization Form to

Release Health Information Needed for Litigation

This form is the product of a collaborative process between the New York State Office of Court Administration, representatives of the medical provider community in New York, and the bench and bar, designed to produce a standard official form that complies with the privacy requirements of the federal Health Insurance Portability and Accountability Act ("HIPAA") and its implementing regulations, to be used to authorize the release of health information needed for litigation in New York State courts. It can, however, be used more broadly than this and be used before litigation has been commenced, or whenever counsel would find it useful.

The goal was to produce a standard HIPAA- compliant official form to obviate the current disputes which often take place as to whether health information requests made in the course of litigation meet the requirements of the HIPAA Privacy Rule. It should be noted, though, that the form is optional. This form may be filled out on line and downloaded to be signed by hand, or downloaded and filled out entirely on paper.

When filing out Item 11, which requests the date or event when the authorization will expire, the person filling out the form may designate an event such as "at the conclusion of my court case" or provide a specific date amount of time, such as "3 years from this date".

If a patient seeks to authorize the release of his or her entire medical record, but only from a certain date, the first two boxes in section 9(a) should both be checked, and the relevant date inserted on the first line containing the first box.

AIDS Law

APPENDIX 33:
TABLE OF STATE STATUTES CONCERNING CRIMINAL TRANSMISSION OF HIV/AIDS

STATE	STATUTE/TYPE OF CRIME
ALABAMA	ALA Code 22-11A-21 (Class C misdemeanor)
ALASKA	NONE
ARIZONA	NONE
ARKANSAS	Ark. Code Ann. 5-14-123 (Class A felony)/ Ark. Code Ann. 20-15-903 (Class A misdemeanor)
CALIFORNIA	Cal. Health & Saf. Code 120291 (Felony punishable by imprisonment for 3,5 or 8 years)/ Cal. Health & Saf. Code 120290 (Misdemeanor) / Cal. Health & Saf. Code 1621.5 (Felony punishable by imprisonment for 2, 4 or 6 years)/ Cal. Pen. Code 12022.85 (3 year sentencing enhancement)
COLORADO	Colo. Rev. Stat. 18-7-201.7 (Class 5 felony) / Colo. Rev. Stat. 18-7-205.7 (Class 6 felony)
CONNECTICUT	NONE
DELAWARE	NONE
DISTRICT OF COLUMBIA	NONE
FLORIDA	Fla. Stat. Ann. 384.24 / Fla. Stat. Ann. 381.0041 (11)(b) (3rd Degree Felony)

STATE	STATUTE/TYPE OF CRIME
GEORGIA	Ga. Code Ann. 16-5-60(c) (Felony punishable by imprisonment for not more than 10 years) / Ga. Code Ann. 16-5-60(d) (Felony punishable by imprisonment for not less than 5 and not more than 20 years)
HAWAII	NONE
IDAHO	Idaho Code 39-608 (Felony punishable by imprisonment for a period not to exceed 15 years or by fine not in excess of $5,000 or by both)
ILLINOIS	Ill. Comp. Stat. 5/12-16.2 (Class 2 felony)
ILLINOIS	III. Ann. Stat. Ch. 20, § 2310/55.45
INDIANA	Ind. Code Ann. 35-42-1-7 (Class C felony for committing the act; Class A felony if the act results in transmission of HIV) / Ind. Code Ann. 35-42-2-6(c) (Class D felony for committing the act; Class C felony if the defendant knew or recklessly failed to know that the bodily fluid or waste was infected with Hepatitis B, HIV or TB; Class B felony if the person knew or recklessly failed to know that the fluid or waste was infected with Hepatitis B or TB and the offense results in transmission; Class A felony if the person knew or recklessly failed to know that the bodily fluid or waste was infected with HIV and the offense resulted in transmission) / Ind. Code Ann. 35-42-2-6(d) (Class D felony if they person knew or recklessly failed to know that the blood, semen, urine or fecal waste was infected with Hepatitis B, HIV or TB; Class C felony if the person knew or recklessly failed to know that the blood, semen, urine, or fecal waste was infected with Hepatitis B or TB and the act results in transmission; Class B felony if the person knew or recklessly failed to know that the blood, semen, urine, or fecal waste was infected with HIV and transmission resulted.
IOWA	Iowa Code 709 C (Class B felony)
KANSAS	NONE
KENTUCKY	Ky. Rev. Stat. 529.090 (Class D felony) / Ky. Rev. Stat. 311.990 (Class D felony)
LOUISIANA	La. Rev. Stat. 43.5 (Fined not more than $5,000 or imprisoned for not more than 11 years or both; if the victim is a police officer acting in the line of duty then the fine increases by $1,000)
MAINE	NONE

STATE	STATUTE/TYPE OF CRIME
MARYLAND	Md. Code Ann. Health-General 18-601 (Fine of $2,500 or imprisonment not exceeding 3 years or both)
MASSACHUSETTS	NONE
MICHIGAN	Mich. Comp. Laws 333.5210 (Felony)
MINNESOTA	NONE
MISSISSIPPI	NONE
MISSOURI	Mo. Rev. Stat 191.677 (Class B felony; Class A felony if transmission occurs)
MONTANA	Mont. Code Ann. 50-18-112 (Misdemeanor)
NEBRASKA	NONE
NEVADA	Nev. Rev. Stat. 201.205 (Category B felony punishable by imprisonment for not less than 2 years and not more than 10 years or by a fine of not more than $10,000 or both) / Nev. Rev. Stat 201.358 (Category B felony punishable by imprisonment for not less than 2 years and not more than 10 years or by a fine of not more than $10,000 or both)
NEW HAMPSHIRE	NONE
NEW JERSEY	N.J. Stat. 2C:34-5 (3rd degree crime)
NEW MEXICO	NONE
NEW YORK	NY Public Health Law 2307 (Misdemeanor)
NORTH CAROLINA	NONE
NORTH DAKOTA	N.D. Cent. Code 12-1-20-17 (Class A felony)
OHIO	Ohio Rev. Code Ann. 2927.13 (Fourth Degree felony)
OKLAHOMA	Okla. Stat. 1192.1 (Felony punishable by imprisonment for not more than 5 years) / Okla. Stat. 1031 (Felony punishable by imprisonment for not more than 5 years) / Okla. Stat. 1-519 (Felony)
OREGON	NONE
PENNSYLVANIA	18 Pa. Cons. Stat. 2703 (2nd degree felony) / 18 Pa. Cons. Stat. 2704 (Penalty shall be the same for murder in the 2nd degree) / 18 Pa. Cons. Stat. 5902(a) (Felony of the 3rd degree) / 18 Pa. Cons. Stat. 5902(b) (Felony of the 3rd degree) / 18 Pa. Cons. Stat. 5902(e) (Felony of the 3rd degree)
RHODE ISLAND	NONE

STATE	STATUTE/TYPE OF CRIME
SOUTH CAROLINA	S.C. Code Ann. 44-29-145 (Felony punishable by fine of not more than $5,000 or imprisonment for not more than 10 years)
SOUTH DAKOTA	S.D Codified Laws 22-18-31 (Class 3 felony)
TENNESSEE	Tenn. Code Ann. 39-13-109 (Class C felony) / Tenn. Code Ann. 68-10-107 (Class C misdemeanor)
TEXAS	NONE
UTAH	Utah Code Ann 76-10-1309 (Felony of the third degree)
VERMONT	NONE
VIRGINIA	Va. Code Ann. 18.2-67, 4:1(A) (Class 6 felony) / Va. Code Ann. 18.2-67, 4:1(B) (Class 1 misdemeanor) / Va. Code Ann. 32.1-289.2 (Class 6 felony)
WASHINGTON	NONE
WEST VIRGINIA	NONE
WISCONSIN	NONE
WYOMING	NONE

Source: American Civil Liberties Union (ACLU) (2005)

APPENDIX 34:
THE NEEDLESTICK SAFETY AND PREVENTION ACT
[Pub.L. No. 106-430, 11/6/2000]

SECTION 1. SHORT TITLE.

This Act may be cited as the "Needlestick Safety and Prevention Act".

SECTION 2. FINDINGS.

The Congress finds the following:

(1) Numerous workers who are occupationally exposed to bloodborne pathogens have contracted fatal and other serious viruses and diseases, including the human immunodeficiency virus (HIV), hepatitis B, and hepatitis C from exposure to blood and other potentially infectious materials in their workplace.

(2) In 1991 the Occupational Safety and Health Administration issued a standard regulating occupational exposure to bloodborne pathogens, including the human immunodeficiency virus, (HIV), the hepatitis B virus (HBV), and the hepatitis C virus (HCV).

(3) Compliance with the bloodborne pathogens standard has significantly reduced the risk that workers will contract a bloodborne disease in the course of their work.

(4) Nevertheless, occupational exposure to bloodborne pathogens from accidental sharps injuries in health care settings continues to be a serious problem. In March 2000, the Centers for Disease Control and Prevention estimated that more than 380,000 percutaneous injuries

from contaminated sharps occur annually among healthcare workers in United States hospital settings. Estimates for all health care settings are that 600,000 to 800,000 needlestick and other percutaneous injuries occur among health care workers annually. Such injuries can involve needles or other sharps contaminated with bloodborne pathogens, such as HIV, HBV, or HCV.

(5) Since publication of the bloodborne pathogens standard in 1991 there has been a substantial increase in the number and assortment of effective engineering controls available to employers. There is now a large body of research and data concerning the effectiveness of newer engineering controls, including safer medical devices.

(6) 396 interested parties responded to a Request for Information (in this section referred to as the "RFI") conducted by the Occupational Safety and Health Administration in 1998 on engineering and work practice controls used to eliminate or minimize the risk of occupational exposure to bloodborne pathogens due to percutaneous injuries from contaminated sharps. Comments were provided by health care facilities, groups representing healthcare workers, researchers, educational institutions, professional and industry associations, and manufacturers of medical devices.

(7) Numerous studies have demonstrated that the use of safer medical devices, such as needleless systems and sharps with engineered sharps injury protections, when they are part of an overall bloodborne pathogens risk-reduction program, can be extremely effective in reducing accidental sharps injuries.

(8) In March 2000, the Centers for Disease Control and Prevention estimated that, depending on the type of device used and the procedure involved, 62 to 88 percent of sharps injuries can potentially be prevented by the use of safer medical devices.

(9) The OSHA 200 Log, as it is currently maintained, does not sufficiently reflect injuries that may involve exposure to bloodborne pathogens in healthcare facilities. More than 98 percent of healthcare facilities responding to the RFI have adopted surveillance systems in addition to the OSHA 200 Log. Information gathered through these surveillance systems is commonly used for hazard identification and evaluation of program and device effectiveness.

(10) Training and education in the use of safer medical devices and safer work practices are significant elements in the prevention of percutaneous exposure incidents. Staff involvement in the device selection and evaluation process is also an important element to achieving a

reduction in sharps injuries, particularly as new safer devices are introduced into the work setting.

(11) Modification of the bloodborne pathogens standard is appropriate to set forth in greater detail its requirement that employers identify, evaluate, and make use of effective safer medical devices.

SECTION 3. BLOODBORNE PATHOGENS STANDARD.

The bloodborne pathogens standard published at 29 CFR 1910.1030 shall be revised as follows:

(1) The definition of "Engineering Controls" (at 29 CFR 1910.1030(b)) shall include as additional examples of controls the following: "safer medical devices, such as sharps with engineered sharps injury protections and needleless systems."

(2) The term "Sharps with Engineered Sharps Injury Protections" shall be added to the definitions (at 29 CFR 1910.1030(b)) and defined as "a nonneedle sharp or a needle device used for withdrawing body fluids, accessing a vein or artery, or administering medications or other fluids, with a built-in safety feature or mechanism that effectively reduces the risk of an exposure incident."

(3) The term "Needleless Systems" shall be added to the definitions (at 29 CFR 1910.1030(b)) and defined as "a device that does not use needles for: (A) the collection of bodily fluids or withdrawal of body fluids after initial venous or arterial access is established; (B) the administration of medication or fluids; or (C) any other procedure involving the potential for occupational exposure to bloodborne pathogens due to percutaneous injuries from contaminated sharps."

(4) In addition to the existing requirements concerning exposure control plans (29 CFR 1910.1030(c)(1)(iv)), the review and update of such plans shall be required to also--

(A) "reflect changes in technology that eliminate or reduce exposure to bloodborne pathogens"; and

(B) "document annually consideration and implementation of appropriate commercially available and effective safer medical devices designed to eliminate or minimize occupational exposure."

(5) The following additional recordkeeping requirement shall be added to the bloodborne pathogens standard at 29 CFR 1910.1030(h):

"The employer shall establish and maintain a sharps injury log for the recording of percutaneous injuries from contaminated sharps.

The information in the sharps injury log shall be recorded and maintained in such manner as to protect the confidentiality of the injured employee. The sharps injury log shall contain, at a minimum—

"(A) the type and brand of device involved in the incident,

"(B) the department or work area where the exposure incident occurred, and

"(C) an explanation of how the incident occurred."

The requirement for such sharps injury log shall not apply to any employer who is not required to maintain a log of occupational injuries and illnesses under 29 CFR 1904 and the sharps injury log shall be maintained for the period required by 29 CFR 1904.6.

(6) The following new section shall be added to the bloodborne pathogens standard: "An employer, who is required to establish an Exposure Control Plan shall solicit input from non-managerial employees responsible for direct patient care who are potentially exposed to injuries from contaminated sharps in the identification, evaluation, and selection of effective engineering and work practice controls and shall document the solicitation in the Exposure Control Plan."

SECTION 4. EFFECT OF MODIFICATIONS.

The modifications under section 3 shall be in force until superseded in whole or in part by regulations promulgated by the Secretary of Labor under section 6(b) of the Occupational Safety and Health Act of 1970 (29 U.S.C. 655(b)) and shall be enforced in the same manner and to the same extent as any rule or regulation promulgated under section 6(b).

SECTION 5. PROCEDURE AND EFFECTIVE DATE.

(a) PROCEDURE- The modifications of the bloodborne pathogens standard prescribed by section 3 shall take effect without regard to the procedural requirements applicable to regulations promulgated under section 6(b) of the Occupational Safety and Health Act of 1970 (29 U.S.C. 655(b)) or the procedural requirements of chapter 5 of title 5, United States Code.

(b) EFFECTIVE DATE- The modifications to the bloodborne pathogens standard required by section 3 shall—

(1) within 6 months of the date of the enactment of this Act, be made and published in the Federal Register by the Secretary of Labor acting through the Occupational Safety and Health Administration; and

(2) at the end of 90 days after such publication, take effect.

Speaker of the House of Representatives.

Vice President of the United States and

President of the Senate.

APPENDIX 35:
NUMBER OF HIV/AIDS CASES
IN STATE AND FEDERAL PRISONS
(YEAR END 2005)

STATE	TOTAL HIV/AIDS CASES
ALABAMA	268
ALASKA	N/A
ARIZONA	152
ARKANSAS	94
CALIFORNIA	1,249
COLORADO	148
CONNECTICUT	463
DELAWARE	124
DISTRICT OF COLUMBIA	N/A
FLORIDA	3,396
GEORGIA	1,042
HAWAII	23
IDAHO	26
ILLINOIS	474
INDIANA	134
IOWA	28
KANSAS	34

STATE	TOTAL HIV/AIDS CASES
KENTUCKY	83
LOUISIANA	488
MAINE	10
MARYLAND	671
MASSACHUSETTS	221
MICHIGAN	525
MINNESOTA	41
MISSISSIPPI	302
MISSOURI	301
MONTANA	6
NEBRASKA	19
NEVADA	124
NEW HAMPSHIRE	21
NEW JERSEY	540
NEW MEXICO	25
NEW YORK	4,440
NORTH CAROLINA	718
NORTH DAKOTA	2
OHIO	410
OKLAHOMA	136
OREGON	N/A
PENNSYLVANIA	692
RHODE ISLAND	58
SOUTH CAROLINA	489
SOUTH DAKOTA	14
TENNESSEE	210
TEXAS	2,400
UTAH	38
VERMONT	11

STATE	TOTAL HIV/AIDS CASES
VIRGINIA	N/A
WASHINGTON	107
WEST VIRGINIA	2
WISCONSIN	122
WYOMING	7
UNITED STATES	22,480

Source: U.S. Department of Justice, Bureau of Justice Statistics

GLOSSARY

Acquired Immune Deficiency Syndrome—An illness characterized by a severe manifestation of infection accompanying the human immunodeficiency virus (HIV).

Acquired Immunity—Immunity acquired by vaccination or exposure of the individual to the infectious agent.

Acute Disease—A disease of sudden onset and relatively short duration.

Acyclovir—An antiviral agent.

AIDS—The acronym for acquired immune deficiency syndrome.

AIDS-Associated Retrovirus (ARV)—Term given the HIV by researchers at the University of California at San Francisco.

AIDS-Related Complex (ARC)—A variety of chronic symptoms and physical findings that occur in some persons who are infected with the HIV but do not meet the Centers for Disease Control's definition of AIDS.

Anemia—A condition characterized by a reduction in the number of red blood cells.

Antibiotic—A drug used to fight bacterial infection.

Antibodies—A special class of proteins produced in response to exposure to specific foreign molecules that neutralize toxins and interact with other components of the immune system to eliminate infectious microorganisms from the body.

Antigen—A foreign substance that is capable of producing an immune response in human beings.

Attending Physician—The doctor who is the primary care giver for a particular patient.

Asymptomatic—Exhibiting no symptoms.

Autoimmune Disease—A condition in which the body's immune system attacks its own tissues.

Autologous Transfusion—A transfusion of one's own blood that was drawn and predeposited prior to the time needed.

Azidothymidine (AZT)—The generic name of the first pharmaceutical licensed by the FDA for the treatment of AIDS.

Biopsy—The removal of a tissue sample for examination.

Blood count—A laboratory test used to determine the number of red cells, white cells and platelets present in the blood.

B-Lymphocytes—Also known as "B cells," refers to a special category of white blood cells originating in the bone marrow that produce antibodies in response to stimulation by antigens.

Cancer—A disease characterized by the growth of abnormal cells that destroy surrounding tissues and can spread to other areas of the body.

Candida Albicans—A fungus causing an oral infection.

Cardiopulmonary Resuscitation (CPR)—Measures designed to restore cardiac function or to support ventilation in the event of a cardiac or respiratory arrest, such as manual chest compression, mouth-to-mouth rescue breathing, intubation, direct cardiac injection, intravenous medications, electrical defibrillation and open-chest cardiac massage

Casual Contact—Refers to ordinary day-to-day interaction between HIV carriers and others.

CD4 Lymphocyte—Also known as a "CD4 T Cell," refers to a helper/inducer lymphocyte that assists in regulating the human immune system and is believed to be the primary target for infection by HIV.

CD8 Lymphocyte—Also known as a"CD8 T Cell," refers to a suppressor lymphocyte that is believed to play important regulatory and functional roles in the human immune system.

CDC—Acronym for the Centers for Disease Control.

Centers for Disease Control (CDC)—U.S. Public Health Service institutions located in Atlanta, Georgia that are concerned with the identification and control of all diseases in the United States.

Chemotherapy—A course of therapy using anticancer drugs.

Chronic Carrier State—An infectious condition in which an infected person or animal does not appear to be sick, but is nonetheless infectious and can transmit the virus to another person or animal.

Chronic Disease—A disease of gradual onset and prolonged duration.

Co-factor—A secondary factor that might contribute to the infectivity of an infectious agent or the spread of the disease caused by that agent.

Cognitive Functions—The mental processes including comprehension, judgment, memory and reasoning.

Comatose—A deep, prolonged unconsciousness usually resulting from injury, disease or poisoning.

Contact Tracing—The interrogation of a person infected with a venereal disease concerning those individuals with whom the infected person has had sexual contact for the purpose of contact and treatment to limit additional exposure.

Decedent—A deceased person.

Dementia—Deterioration of an individual's mental state due to organic brain disease.

DNA—Acronym for deoxyribonucleic acid found principally within the nuclei of cells that affects the transmittal of hereditary traits, including HIV.

Do Not Resuscitate Order—A notation in the patient's medical record that cardiopulmonary resuscitation should not be undertaken in the event the patient suffers cardiac or respiratory arrest.

ELISA—Acronym for enzyme linked immuno-sorbent assay which is a test employed initially to screen antibodies to the AIDS virus.

Epidemiology—The science of studying the transmission of disease.

Epstein-Barr Virus—A member of the herpes group of viruses and the principal cause of infectious mononucleosis in young adults.

Etiology—The study of the causes and mechanisms of disease.

False Negative—A negative reaction in a test that should have been positive.

False Positive—A positive reaction in a test that should have been negative.

Hemophilia—An inherited disorder occurring almost exclusively in males that is associated with a deficiency in one or more blood-clotting factors.

Hepatitis—Inflammation of the liver characterized by jaundice, vomiting, malaise, fever and abdominal pain.

Herpes Simplex—An acute disease caused by certain types of herpes viruses, characterized by painful blisters on the skin and mucous membranes. Herpes Simplex I refers to the virus that commonly causes cold sores on the mouth and face. Herpes Simplex II refers to a sexually transmitted virus that commonly causes painful sores in the anal and genital area.

High-Risk Individual—Persons at high risk of contracting HIV, including homosexual or bisexual men, intravenous drug abusers, prostitutes, hemophiliacs, or the sexual partners of any of the foregoing.

HIV—Acronym for the human immunodeficiency virus which causes AIDS.

Immune Response—Response of the human body to a foreign substance with the development of antibodies and other substances that may reverse the infection and prevent subsequent infection by the same organism.

Immune System—The system that defends the human body against invasion by infectious and other foreign agents.

Immunity—A condition during which the human body is capable of neutralizing a foreign substances and preventing the latter from causing an adverse reaction in that individual.

Incidence of Disease—The percentage of individuals infected with a particular disease within a defined population in a given period of time, as set forth by the Centers for Disease Control.

Incubation Period—The interval between the time the individual contracts an infection and the onset of overt signs and symptoms of the infection.

Innate Immunity—Immunity acquired at conception or during intrauterine development.

Interferon—A complex protein believed to be produced or released by human cells following a viral infection that has been used as a treatment for AIDS.

Interleukin-2—Also known as the "T-cell growth factor," refers to a substance produced by T lymphocytes that stimulates activated T lymphocytes and some activated B-lymphocytes to proliferate.

Intravenous—Into a vein.

Kaposi's Sarcoma—A vascular tumor that appears as a blue-violet to brownish cutaneous lesion.

Lymph Nodes—Glands that fight infection by producing antibodies and filtering out germs.

Mortality Rate—Ratio of the number of deaths to a given population.

Opportunistic Infection—An infection caused by a microorganism that rarely causes disease in persons with normal defense mechanisms.

Parenteral—Refers to introduction into the bloodstream.

Prevalence—Refers to the total number of cases of a disease in existence at a particular time in a specified area.

Provirus—A copy of the genetic information of an animal virus that is integrated into the DNA of an infected cell.

PWA—Acronym for "person with AIDS."

Red Blood Cells—The blood cells which carry oxygen.

Retrovirus—A class of viruses that contain the genetic material RNA and have the capability to copy this RNA into DNA inside an infected cell, thus incorporating the DNA into the genetic structure of the cell in the form of a provirus.

RNA—Acronym for ribonucleic acid, a nucleic acid associated with the control of chemical activities inside a cell.

Safe Sex—Sexual practices designed to prevent the exchange of body fluids and thereby limit the opportunity for HIV transmission.

Sensitivity—As it pertains to serologic testing, refers to the percentage of people who test positive and in fact have the condition for which they were tested.

Seropositive—As it pertains to HIV testing, refers to the condition in which antibodies to the virus are found in the blood.

Sexually Transmitted Disease (STD)—Diseases commonly transmitted through sexual activity including AIDS, herpes, syphilis and gonorrhea.

Statute—A law.

STD—Acronym for sexually transmitted disease.

T Lymphocyte—Also known as a "T Cell," refers to a cell that matures in the thymus gland and is found primarily in the blood, lymph and lymphoid organs.

T4 Lymphocyte—Also known as a "T4 Cell," it is synonymous with the CD4 T Cell.

T8 Lymphocyte—Also known as a "T8 Cell," it is synonymous with the CD8 T Cell.

Terminal Illness—An incurable condition caused by injury, disease or illness which, regardless of the application of life-sustaining procedures would, within reasonable medical judgment, produce death and where the application of life-sustaining procedures serve only to postpone the moment of death of the patient.

Transfusion—The injection of blood or blood products directly into the bloodstream.

Vaccine—A preparation consisting of an infectious agent which is administered to stimulate the development of defense mechanisms by the body's immune system.

Western Blot Technique—A test that identifies antibodies against specific protein molecules and which is more complex and expansive than the ELISA test, but thought to be more precise in detecting antibodies to HIV in blood samples.

White Blood Cells—The blood cells that make up the immune system, also known as leukocytes.

BIBLIOGRAPHY AND ADDITIONAL READING

American Civil Liberties Union (ACLU) Department of Public Education (Date Visited: February 2008) http://www.aclu.org/.

American Health Lawyers Association (Date Visited: February 2008) http://www.healthlawyers.org/.

Avert (Date Visited: February 2008) http://www.avert.org/.

Black's Law Dictionary, Fifth Edition. St. Paul, MN: West Publishing Company, 1979.

Business and Labor Resource Service (Date Visited: February 2008) http://www.hivatwork.org/.

Centers for Disease Control and Prevention (Date Visited: February 2008) http://www.cdc.gov/.

Cincinnati STD/HIV Prevention Training Center Network (Date Visited: February 2008) http://stdptc.uc.edu/.

Department of Health and Human Services (Date Visited February 2008) http://www.hhs.gov/.

Kaiser State Health Facts (Date Visited: February 2008) http://www.statehealthfacts.org/.

Names Project Foundation (Date Visited: February 2008) http://aidsquilt.org/.

National Center for HIV, STD and TB Prevention (NCHSTP) (Date Visited: February 2008) http://www.cdc.gov/nchhstp/.

New York State Department of Health (Date Visited: February 2008) http://www.health.state.ny.us/nysdoh/hivaids/.

San Francisco AIDS Foundation (Date Visited: February 2008) http:// www.sfaf.org/.

UNAIDS (Date Visited: February 2008) http://www.unaids.org/.

U.S. Department of Justice, Bureau of Justice Statistics (Date Visited: February 2008) http://www.ojp.usdoj.gov/bjs/.

U.S. Department of Veterans Affairs (Date Visited: February 2008) http://www.hiv.va.gov/.